The Sil\

Sean O'Casey was born in Dublin in 1880. He was the youngest of thirteen children and, because of malnutrition, ill health and poverty, he had little formal education. Although the first half of his life was spent as a labourer, he involved himself with the Irish political struggle both for independence and the betterment of conditions for the poor. He was secretary of the Irish Citizen Army, and wrote for *The Irish Worker*. The production at the Abbey Theatre of his early plays translated his experiences into art and brought him international acclaim. Like many another great Irish writer, he paid his country the compliment of leaving it as soon as he conveniently could. For many years he made his home in Devon, where he died in 1964.

SEAN O'CASEY

The Silver Tassie

A TRAGI-COMEDY IN FOUR ACTS

FABER & FABER

This edition first published in 2014
by Faber and Faber Limited
74–77 Great Russell Street, London WC1B 3DA

First published by Macmillan London Ltd in 1928
Reprinted in *Sean O'Casey: Plays Two*
by Faber and Faber Limited, 1998

Typeset by Country Setting, Kingsdown, Kent CT14 8ES
Printed and bound by CPI Group (UK) Ltd, Croydon, CR0 4YY

A CIP record for this book
is available from the British Library

ISBN 978-0-571-31518-5

FSC
www.fsc.org
MIX
Paper from
responsible sources
FSC® C101712

2 4 6 8 10 9 7 5 3 1

Introduction

JAMES MORAN

In the mid-1920s, Sean O'Casey made his name by writing a trio of plays that are all set in Dublin's tenements at different points during the Irish revolution of 1916–23. These plays were premiered at Dublin's Abbey Theatre, and enjoyed immediate critical and commercial success. In 1923 the *Dublin Evening Herald* declared O'Casey's debut work, *The Shadow of a Gunman*, to be 'brilliant, truthful, decisive' and 'flawless'. In 1925 his next play, *Juno and the Paycock*, won the Hawthornden literary prize, and in 1926 the *Irish Times* described the premiere of O'Casey's third major play, *The Plough and the Stars*, as 'the high-water mark of public interest in the work of the Abbey Theatre'. The *Plough and the Stars* had nonetheless angered some nationalists, who rioted in response to that production and helped trigger O'Casey's decision to move to London. Here he was visited by two of the Abbey Theatre directors, W.B. Yeats and Lennox Robinson, who implored him to send his next play to the Abbey: he promised and did.

In March 1928 the author was known to have submitted a new script to the Abbey, and Dublin anticipated another triumph. O'Casey had proven himself capable of writing with insight and inventiveness about the way that residents of Dublin had been affected by wartime. The new play, *The Silver Tassie*, would deal with the First World War (the conflict that had preceded and triggered those which his other plays had described) and would begin in the domestic apartments of Dublin, thus potentially extending his well-received trilogy into a tetralogy. In April 1928 the *Irish Times* excitedly reported that 'friends of Mr O'Casey who have been privileged to read his new play have passed high opinions on its merits, and its production is being eagerly awaited'. Indeed, O'Casey received words of encouragement from the playhouse as he completed and submitted the work, with one of the theatre's directors, Lady Gregory, writing, 'I long to see it – I'm sure the wine you have filled it with is of the best vintage'. In fact, O'Casey felt so sure that the Abbey would produce the work that he even submitted a suggested cast list along with the script.

However, for O'Casey disaster then struck. The Abbey rejected the play. Notoriously, the theatre's founding director W.B. Yeats guided the managerial decision, and wrote a high-handed letter to O'Casey declaring: 'You are not interested in the Great War; you never stood on its battlefields or walked its hospitals, and so write out of your opinions. You illustrate those opinions by a series of almost unrelated scenes as you might in a leading article'.

O'Casey felt distressed by this dismissal, and he had good reason to feel upset. The rejection letter failed even to spell his name correctly, even though his plays had bankrolled the Abbey Theatre during recent lean years. In fact, his earlier work, *The Plough and the Stars*, was being revived at the Abbey at exactly the same time that the directors were rejecting O'Casey's new play, meaning that the audience's appreciation for O'Casey was literally ringing in the directors' ears as they turned down his latest effort. One of the directors wrote to O'Casey to say, 'I return the M.S. of *The Silver Tassie*. As I write this I hear the audience cheering *The Plough*.'

In a fit of pique at Yeats's behaviour – particularly Yeats's 'face saving' suggestion that O'Casey himself should withdraw the play in order to rewrite it – O'Casey decided to publish all the related correspondence about the rejection in the *Observer* and the *Irish Times*, bringing public attention to the spat. Yeats felt so shocked by this indiscretion that he took to his bed for two days. But the decision to publish that material caused most long-term damage to O'Casey himself. His play *The Silver Tassie* would long be associated with Yeats's harsh words and with that 1928 verdict that the script is not stageworthy. Since then it has rarely been grouped with the earlier three plays, and has been seen on stage far less frequently.

So why had Yeats led his fellow directors in declining *The Silver Tassie*? Well, there may have been some professional rivalry involved, as Yeats himself worked as a playwright and his dramas had tanked at the Abbey box office during O'Casey's period of success. But, more fundamentally, Yeats had deep misgivings about the whole idea of literary writers tackling the topic of the world war. When Yeats edited the 1936 *Oxford Book of Modern Verse* he consciously omitted the war poets, famously explaining that 'passive suffering is not a theme for poetry'. So many people had grown obsessed by military conflict, but Yeats declared, 'I give it as little thought as I can.'

O'Casey, by contrast, gave the war a great deal of thought, and felt exasperated by Yeats's attitude. O'Casey had never seen action, but he knew a great deal about the conflict's victims. During 1915 he had needed surgery on tubercular glands in his neck, and found himself admitted to St Vincent's Hospital in Dublin, which had been commandeered as a field hospital. Here O'Casey witnessed at first hand the sufferings of the gassed, the shell-shocked, and the maimed. In particular, O'Casey saw the sad way that his own surgeon at the hospital, Richard Tobin, had been deeply affected by the recent death of a son. The younger Tobin was a talented Dublin sportsman whose prowess had often been described in the Irish newspapers and who had played in a rugby team representing his father's hospital in 1914, but who had then enlisted in a 'pals' battalion' and died at the Dardanelles. This tale, and other terrible stories, circulated on the wards that O'Casey inhabited during 1915, preparing the way for *The Silver Tassie*'s tragic narrative.

Yeats preferred literary writers to keep the war in the background, but also disliked the theatrical style that O'Casey was now developing. O'Casey wanted to avoid being defined by what drama critic Huntley Carter had called 'stark realism', and felt increasingly fascinated by theatrical expressionism. In 1925 O'Casey had seen a performance of the play *Masse Mensch* by the German expressionist Ernst Toller, which proceeds by alternating episodes that advance the story with dream scenes that develop the meaning and significance of the action. In *The Silver Tassie* an admiring O'Casey attempted to do something similar, and so his first-act realism moves into a fantastical second act where he sought to develop the meaning of the opening section by abandoning the naturalistic setting as well as all the characters he had just introduced.

For Yeats, this had simply made *The Silver Tassie* into an incoherent mish-mash. But that opinion was contradicted by the English theatrical manager Charles Cochran, who declared that the second act was 'without exception the finest symbolic scene I can recall', and sunk £5,000 of his own money into a London production. *The Silver Tassie* therefore became the first O'Casey play to be premiered outside Dublin when it was first staged at London's Apollo Theatre in 1929, although in retrospect this may not have been the most strategically brilliant venue in which to perform O'Casey's new work. Staging *The Silver Tassie* at the Apollo inevitably invited comparisons with R.C. Sherriff's smash-hit First World War drama *Journey's End*, which had premiered with Laurence Olivier at the same London playhouse only ten months previously. In his personal collection of press cuttings, O'Casey kept and highlighted the *Daily Sketch*'s hostile review of *The Silver Tassie*, which compared his sprawling, expressionist montage in an unflattering way to the tight and realistic depiction of the trenches that can be found in Sherriff's work.

Nonetheless, from today's perspective we can recognise the prescient and forward-looking aspects of O'Casey's drama. With its crazy shifts of time and tone, refusal of easy religious consolations, and contrasts between the sacrifice of the front and the comforts of the civilian, O'Casey's play anticipates the celebrated theatrical style of Theatre Workshop's *Oh What a Lovely War* (1963). In his clear-eyed focus on the destructive futility of the conflict, O'Casey was also predicting the political viewpoint of that play and of *Blackadder Goes Forth* (1989), a viewpoint that continues to provoke bewilderment and anger among British politicians and journalists in our own day.

Meanwhile, in the late 1920s, those who ran the Abbey Theatre very quickly realised that they had made a mistake with *The Silver Tassie*. Soon after the rejection letter had been sent to O'Casey, one of the Abbey board members had broken ranks and told the press that 'I should like to see it on the stage'. Lady Gregory then travelled to watch the London production, and noted sadly in her diary that the Abbey really should have produced the drama. Within the next decade, even a repentant Yeats had realised the merits of O'Casey's text, and asked for permission to stage it at the Abbey, where it was produced in 1935. The Abbey Theatre and O'Casey were both damaged by the brouhaha over the rejection, but, to this day, the play itself remains a most perceptive Irish account of the poetry and the pity of the First World War.

James Moran is currently a mid-career fellow of the British Academy and associate professor in English at the University of Nottingham. His book The Theatre of Sean O'Casey *was published by Bloomsbury in 2013.*

The Silver Tassie was first performed at the Apollo
Theatre, London, on 11 October 1929. The cast, in order
of appearance, was as follows:

Sylvester Heegan Barry Fitzgerald
Simon Norton Sydney J. Morgan
Mrs Heegan Eithne Magee
Susie Monican Beatrix Lehmann
Mrs Foran Una O'Connor
Teddy Foran Ian Hunter
Harry Heegan Charles Laughton
Jessie Taite Billy Barnes
Barney Bagnall S.J. Warrington
The Croucher Leonard Shepherd
First Soldier Charles Laughton
Second Soldier Ian Hunter
Third Soldier Barry Fitzgerald
Fourth Soldier Jack Mayne
Fifth Soldier G. Adrian Byrne
Fourth Stretcher-Bearer Barry Barnes
The Corporal Sinclair Cotter
The Visitor Ivo Dawson
The Staff Wallah Alban Blakelock
The Trumpeter Emlyn Williams
First Stretcher-Bearer Norman Stuart
Second Stretcher-Bearer Oswald Lingard
Third Stretcher-Bearer Charles Schofield
First Casualty Clive Morton
Second Casualty James Willoughby
Surgeon Forby Maxwell Hastings Lynn
Sister of the Ward Audrey O'Flynn

Director Raymond Massey
Settings by Augustus John
Produced by Charles Cochrane

The first performance in Ireland was at the Abbey
Theatre, Dublin, in 1935, directed by Arthur Shields and
with settings based on original designs by Maurice
McGonigal.

The Silver Tassie was revived at the Aldwych Theatre, London, by the Royal Shakespeare Company on 10 September 1969. The cast was as follows:

Sylvester Heegan David Waller
Mrs Heegan Patience Collier
Simon Norton Clifford Rose
Susie Monican Helen Mirren
Mrs Foran Frances Cuka
Teddy Foran Patrick Stewart
Harry Heegan Richard Moore
Jessie Taite Sara Kestelman
Barney Bagnal Bruce Myers
The Croucher Ben Kingsley
First Soldier John Kane
Second Soldier Bryan Robson
Third Soldier Robert Oates
Fourth Soldier Patrick Stewart
Fifth Soldier David Stern
Sixth Soldier Martin Bax
Corporal Philip Manikum
Visitor Richard Simpson
Staff-Wallah Julian Curry
First Stretcher-Bearer Glynne Lewis
Second Stretcher-Bearer Ralph Cotterill
Third Stretcher-Bearer John York
Fourth Stretcher-Bearer Peter Cochran
Fifth Stretcher-Bearer Stephen Turner
Sixth Stretcher-Bearer Peter Harlowe
First Casualty J.D. Stender
Second Casualty David Firth

Third Casualty Ian Dyson
Dressing Station Attendant David Sadgrove
Surgeon Forby Maxwell Bernard Lloyd
Ward Sister Ruby Head
Conroy Jeremy Barlow

Directed by David Jones
Designed by John Bury

The Silver Tassie was revived on the Lyttelton stage of the National Theatre, London, on 15 April 2014. The cast was as follows:

Sylvester Heegan Aidan McArdle
Simon Norton Stephen Kennedy
Mrs Foran Aoife McMahon
Susie Monican Judith Roddy
Mrs Heegan Josie Walker
Teddy Foran Aidan Kelly
Harry Heegan Ronan Raftery
Jessie Taite Deirdre Mullins
Barney Bagnal Adam Best
The Croucher Benjamin Dilloway
Soldier 1 Sam O'Mahoney
Soldier 2 Jordan Mifsud
Soldier 4 Ronan Raftery
Soldier 1 Aidan Kelly
The Corporal Andrew Westfield
The Visitor George Potts
Staff Wallah Jim Creighton
First Stretcher-Bearer John Cormack
Second Stretcher-Bearer Brendan Fleming
Third Stretcher-Bearer Eoin Geoghegan
Fourth Stretcher-Bearer Fred Lancaster
First Casualty Donnla Hughes
Second Casualty Owen Findlay
Surgeon Forby Maxwell Jim Creighton
Ward Sister Lucia McAnespie

Director Howard Davies
Set Designer Vicki Mortimer
Costume Designer John Bright
Lighting Designer Neil Austin
Music Stephen Warbeck
Choreographer Scarlett Mackmin
Sound Designer Paul Groothuis

Characters

Sylvester Heegan

Mrs Heegan
his wife

Simon Norton

Susie Monican

Mrs Foran

Teddy Foran
her husband

Harry Heegan, DCM
Heegan's son

Jessie Taite

Barney Bagnal

The Croucher

Four Soldiers

The Corporal

The Visitor

The Staff-Wallah

Four Stretcher-Bearers

First Casualty

Second Casualty

Surgeon Forby Maxwell

The Sister of the Ward

Author's Notes

The Croucher's make-up should come as close as possible to a death's head, a skull; and his hands should show like those of a skeleton's. He should sit somewhere above the group of Soldiers; preferably to one side, on the left, from viewpoint of audience, so as to overlook the Soldiers. He should look languid, as if very tired of life.

The group of Soldiers in Act Two should enter in a close mass, as if each was keeping the other from falling, utterly weary and tired out. They should appear as if they were almost locked together.

The Soldiers' last response to the Staff-Wallah's declaration, namely 'To the guns!', should have in these three words the last high notes of 'The Last Post'.

The song sung at the end of the play should be given to the best two (or one) singers in the cast. If, on the other hand, there be no passable singer among the players, the song should be omitted.

Perhaps a more suitable Spiritual than 'Sweet Chariot' would be chosen for Harry to sing. For instance, 'Keep Inchin' Along', or 'Keep Me from Sinkin' Down'.

The chants in the play are simple plain song. The first chant is given in full as an example of the way in which they are sung. In the others, the dots . . . indicate that the note preceding them should be sustained till the music indicates a change. There are three parts in each chant: the Intonation; the Meditation; and the Ending. After a little practice, they will be found to be easy to sing. The Soldiers having the better voices should be selected to intone the chants, irrespective of the numbers allotted to them as characters in the book of the play.

THE SILVER TASSIE

To Eileen
with the yellow daffodils in the green vase

Act One
Room in Heegan's home

Act Two
Somewhere in France (later on)

Act Three
Ward in a hospital (a little later on)

Act Four
Room in premises of Avondale Football Club

Act One

The eating, sitting, and part sleeping room of the Heegan
family. A large window at back looks on to a quay, from
which can be seen the centre mast of a steamer, at the
top of which gleams a white light. Another window at
right looks down on a side street. Under the window at
back, plumb in the centre, is a stand, the legs gilded silver
and the top gilded gold; on the stand is a purple velvet
shield on which are pinned a number of silver medals
surrounding a few gold ones. On each side of the shield
is a small vase holding a bunch of artificial flowers. The
shield is draped with red and yellow ribbons. To the left
of the stand is a bed covered with a bedspread of black
striped with vivid green. To the right of the stand is a
dresser and chest of drawers combined. The fireplace is
to the left. Beside the fireplace is a door leading to a
bedroom, another door which gives access to the rest of
the house and the street, on the right. At the corner left is
a red-coloured stand resembling an easel, having on it a
silver-gilt framed picture photograph of Harry Heegan in
football dress, crimson jersey with yellow collar and cuffs
and a broad yellow belt, black stockings, and yellow
football boots. A table on which are a half-pint bottle of
whiskey, a large parcel of bread and meat sandwiches,
and some copies of English illustrated magazines.

Sylvester Heegan and Simon Norton are sitting by the
fire. Sylvester Heegan is a stockily built man of sixty-five;
he has been a docker all his life since first the muscles of
his arms could safely grip a truck, and even at sixty-five
the steel in them is only beginning to stiffen.

Simon Norton is a tall man, originally a docker too,
but by a little additional steadiness, a minor effort

towards self-education, a natural, but very slight superior nimbleness of mind, has risen in the company's estimation and has been given the position of checker, a job entailing as many hours of work as a docker, almost as much danger, twice as much responsibility, and a corresponding reduction in his earning powers. He is not so warmly, but a little more circumspectly dressed than Sylvester, and in his manner of conduct and speech there is a hesitant suggestion of greater refinement than in those of Sylvester, and a still more vague indication that he is aware of it. This timid semi-conscious sense of superiority, which Simon sometimes forgets, is shown frequently by a complacent stroking of a dark beard which years are beginning to humiliate. The night is cold, and Simon and Sylvester occasionally stretch longingly towards the fire. They are fully dressed and each has his topcoat and hat beside him, as if ready to go out at a moment's notice.

Susie Monican is standing at the table polishing a Lee-Enfield rifle with a chamois cloth; the butt of the rifle is resting on the table. She is a girl of twenty-two, well-shaped limbs, challenging breasts, all of which are defiantly hidden by a rather long dark-blue skirt and bodice buttoning up to the throat, relieved by a crimson scarf around her neck, knotted in front and falling down her bosom like a man's tie. She is undeniably pretty, but her charms are almost completely hidden by her sombre, ill-fitting dress, and the rigid manner in which she has made her hair up declares her unflinching and uncompromising modesty. Just now she is standing motionless, listening intently, looking towards the door on right.

Mrs Heegan is standing at the window at right, listening too, one hand pulling back the curtain, but her attention, taken from the window, is attracted to the door. She is older than Sylvester, stiffened with age and rheumatism; the end of her life is unknowingly lumbering towards a rest: the impetus necessity has given to continual

4

toil and striving is beginning to slow down, and everything she has to do is done with a quiet mechanical persistence. Her inner ear cannot hear even a faint echo of a younger day. Neither Sylvester nor Simon has noticed the attentive attitude of Mrs Heegan or Susie, for Sylvester, with one arm outstretched crooked at the elbow, is talking with subdued intensity to Simon.

Sylvester I seen him do it, mind you. I seen him do it.

Simon I quite believe you, Sylvester.

Sylvester Break a chain across his bisseps! (*With panto-mime action.*) Fixes it over his arm . . . bends it up . . . a little strain . . . snaps in two . . . right across his bisseps!

Susie Shush you, there!

> *Mrs Heegan goes out with troubled steps by door. The rest remain still for a few moments.*

Sylvester A false alarm.

Simon No cause for undue anxiety; there's plenty of time yet.

Susie (*chanting as she resumes the polishing of gun*)
Man walketh in a vain shadow, and disquieteth himself in vain:
He heapeth up riches, and cannot tell who shall gather them.

> *She sends the chant in the direction of Sylvester and Simon, coming close to the two men and sticking an angry face in between them.*

When the two of yous stand quiverin' together on the dhread day of the Last Judgement, how will the two of yous feel if yous have nothin' to say but 'He broke a chain across his bisseps'? Then the two of you'll know that the wicked go down into hell, an' all the people who forget God!

5

She listens a moment, and leaving down the rifle, goes out by door left.

Sylvester It's persecutin', that tambourine theology of Susie's. I always get a curious, sickenin' feelin', Simon, when I hear the Name of the Supreme Bein' tossed into the quietness of a sensible conversation.

Simon The day he won the Cross Country Championship of County Dublin, Syl, was a day to be chronicled.

Sylvester In a minor way, yes, Simon. But the day that caps the chronicle was the one when he punched the fear of God into the heart of Police Constable 63C under the stars of a frosty night on the way home from Terenure.

Simon Without any exaggeration, without any exaggeration, mind you, Sylvester, that could be called a memorable experience.

Sylvester I can see him yet –

He gets up, slides from side to side, dodging and parrying imaginary blows.

– glidin' round the dazzled Bobby, cross-ey'd tryin' to watch him.

Simon (*tapping his pipe resolutely on the hob*) Unperturbed, mind you, all the time.

Sylvester An' the hedges by the roadside standin' stiff in the silent cold of the air, the frost beads on the branches glistenin' like toss'd-down diamonds from the breasts of the stars, the quietness of the night stimulated to a fuller stillness by the mockin' breathin' of Harry, an' the heavy, ragin' pantin' of the Bobby, an' the quickenin' beats of our own hearts afraid, of hopin' too little or hopin' too much.

During the last speech by Sylvester, Susie has come in with a bayonet, and has commenced to polish it.

Susie We don't go down on our knees often enough; that's why we're not able to stand up to the Evil One: we don't go down on our knees enough . . . I can hear some persons fallin' with a splash of sparks into the lake of everlastin' fire . . . An account of every idle word shall be given at the last day.

She goes out again with rifle. Bending towards Simon and Sylvester as she goes:

God is listenin' to yous; God is listenin' to yous!

Sylvester Dtch, dtch, dtch. People ought to be forcibly restrained from constantly cannonadin' you with the name of the Deity.

Simon Dubiety never brush'd a thought into my mind, Syl, while I was waitin' for the moment when Harry would stretch the Bobby hors dee combaa on the ground.

Sylvester (*resuming his pantomime actions*) There he was staggerin', beatin' out blindly, every spark of energy panted out of him, while Harry feinted, dodg'd, side-stepp'd, then suddenly sail'd in an' put him asleep with . . .

Simon ⎤ A right-handed hook to the jaw!

Sylvester ⎦ A left-handed hook to the jaw!

Sylvester (*after a pause*) A left-handed hook to the jaw, Simon.

Simon No, no, Syl, a right-handed hook to the jaw.

Mrs Foran runs quickly in by the door with a frying pan in her hand, on which is a steak. She comes to the fire, pushing, so as to disturb the two men. She is one of the many gay, careworn women of the working class.

Mrs Foran (*rapidly*) A pot of clothes is boilin' on the fire above, an' I knew yous wouldn't mind me slappin' a bit

7

of steak on here for a second to show him, when he comes in before he goes away, that we're mindful of his needs, an' I'm hopeful of a dream tonight that the sea's between us, not lookin' very haggard in the mornin' to find the dream a true one. (*With satisfied anticipation.*)

For I'll be single again, yes, I'll be single again;
An' I eats what I likes, . . . an' I drinks what I likes,
An' I likes what I likes, when I'm –

(*Stopping suddenly.*) What's the silence for?

Sylvester (*slowly and decidedly*) I was at the fight, Simon, an' I seen him givin' a left-handed hook to the jaw.

Mrs Foran What fight?

Simon (*slowly and decidedly*) I was there too, an' I saw him down the Bobby with a right-handed hook to the jaw.

Mrs Foran What Bobby?

A pause.

Sylvester It was a close-up, an' I don't know who'd know better if it wasn't the boy's own father.

Mrs Foran What boy . . . what father?

Sylvester Oh, shut up, woman, an' don't be smotherin' us with a shower of questions.

Susie (*who has entered on the last speech, and has started to polish a soldier's steel helmet*) Oh, the miserableness of them that don't know the things that belong unto their peace. They try one thing after another, they try everything, but they never think of trying God. (*Coming nearer to them.*) Oh, the happiness of knowing that God's hand has pick'd you out for heaven. (*To Mrs Foran.*) What's the honeypot kiss of a lover to the kiss of righteousness and peace?

8

Mrs Foran, embarrassed, goes over to window.

(*Turning to Simon.*) Simon, will you not close the dandy door of the public house and let the angels open the pearly gates of heaven for you?

Sylvester We feel very comfortable where we are, Susie.

Susie Don't mock, Sylvester, don't mock. You'd run before a great wind, tremble in an earthquake, and flee from a fire; so don't treat lightly the still, small voice calling you to repentance and faith.

Sylvester (*with appeal and irritation*) Oh, do give over worryin' a man, Susie.

Susie God shows His love by worrying, and worrying, and worrying the sinner. The day will come when you will call on the mountains to cover you, and then you'll weep and gnash your teeth that you did not hearken to Susie's warning. (*Putting her hands appealingly on his shoulders.*) Sylvester, if you pray long enough, and hard enough, and deep enough, you'll get the power to fight and conquer Beelzebub.

Mrs Foran I'll be in a doxological mood tonight, not because the kingdom of heaven 'll be near me, but because my husband 'll be far away, and tomorrow – (*Singing.*)
  I'll be single again, yes, single again;
  An' I goes where I likes, an' I does what I likes,
  An' I likes what I likes now I'm single again!

Simon Go on getting Harry's things ready, Susie, and defer the dosing of your friends with canticles till the time is ripe with rest for them to listen quietly.

Simon and Sylvester are very self-conscious during Susie's talk to them. Simon empties his pipe by tapping the head on the hob of the grate. He then blows

9

*through it. As he is blowing through it, Sylvester is
emptying his by tapping it on the hob; as he is blowing
it Simon taps his again; as Simon taps Sylvester taps
with him, and then they look into the heads of the
pipes and blow together.*

Susie It must be mercy or it must be judgement: if not
mercy today it may be judgement tomorrow. He is never
tired of waiting and waiting and waiting; and watching
and watching and watching; and knocking and knocking
and knocking for the sinner – you, Sylvester, and you,
Simon – to turn from his wickedness and live. Oh, if the
two of you only knew what it was to live! Not to live
leg-staggering an' belly-creeping among the pain-spotted
and sin-splashed desires of the flesh; but to live, oh, to
live swift-flying from a holy peace to a holy strength, and
from holy strength to a holy joy, like the flashing flights
of a swallow in the deep beauty of a summer sky.

*Simon and Sylvester shift about, self-conscious and
uneasy.*

(*Placing her hand first on Simon's shoulder and then on
Sylvester's.*) The two of you God's elegant swallows; a
saved pair; a loving pair strong-wing'd, freed from the
gin of the snarer, tip of wing to tip of wing, flying fast or
darting swift together to the kingdom of heaven.

Simon (*expressing a protecting thought to Sylvester*) One
of the two of us should go out and hunt back the old
woman from the perishing cold of watching for the
return of Harry.

Sylvester She'll be as cold as a naked corpse, an'
unstinted watchin' won't bring Harry back a minute
sooner. I'll go an' drive her back. (*He rises to go.*) I'll be
back in a minute, Susie.

Simon (*hurriedly*) Don't bother, Syl, I'll go; she won't be
farther than the corner of the street; you go on toasting

yourself where you are. (*He rises.*) I'll be back in a minute, Susie.

Mrs Foran (*running to the door*) Rest easy the two of you, an' I'll go, so as to give Susie full time to take the sin out of your bones an' put you both in first-class form for the kingdom of heaven. (*She goes out.*)

Susie Sinners that jeer often add to the glory of God: going out, she gives you, Sylvester, and you, Simon, another few moments, precious moments – oh, how precious, for once gone, they are gone for ever – to listen to the warning from heaven.

Simon (*suddenly*) Whisht, here's somebody coming, I think?

Sylvester I'll back this is Harry comin' at last.

A pause as the three listen.

No, it's nobody.

Simon Whoever it was 's gone by.

Susie Oh, Syl, oh, Simon, don't try to veil the face of God with an evasion. You can't, you can't cod God. This may be your last chance before the pains of hell encompass the two of you. Hope is passing by; salvation is passing by, and glory arm in arm with her. In the quietness left to you go down on your knees and pray that they come into your hearts and abide with you for ever . . . (*With fervour, placing her left hand on Simon's shoulder and her right hand on Sylvester's, and shaking them.*) Get down on your knees, get down on your knees, get down on your knees and pray for conviction of sin, lest your portion in David become as the portion of the Canaanites, the Amorites, the Perizzites and the Jebusites!

Sylvester Eh, eh, Susie; cautious now – you seem to be forgettin' yourself.

Simon Desist, Susie, desist. Violence won't gather people to God. It only ingenders hostility to what you're trying to do.

Sylvester You can't batter religion into a man like that.

Simon Religion is love, but that sort of thing is simply a nullification of religion.

Susie Bitterness and wrath in exhortation is the only hope of rousing the pair of yous into a sense of coming and everlasting penalties.

Sylvester Well, give it a miss, give it a miss to me now. Don't try to claw me into the kingdom of heaven. An' you only succeed in distempering piety when you try to mangle it into a man's emotions.

Simon Heaven is all the better, Susie, for being a long way off.

Sylvester If I want to pray I do it voluntarily, but I'm not going to be goaded an' goaded into it.

Susie I go away in a few days to help to nurse the wounded, an' God's merciful warnings may depart along with me, then sin 'll usher the two of you into Gehenna for all eternity. Oh, if the two of you could only grasp the meaning of the word eternity! (*Bending down and looking up into their faces.*) Time that had no beginning and never can have an end – an' there you'll be – two cockatrices creeping together, a desolation, an astonishment, a curse and a hissing from everlasting to everlasting. (*She goes into room.*)

Sylvester Cheerful, what! Cockatrices – be-God, that's a good one, Simon.

Simon Always a trying thing to have to listen to one that's trying to push the kingdom of God into a reservation of a few yards.

Sylvester A cockatrice! Now where did she manage to pick up that term of approbation, I wonder?

Simon From the Bible. An animal somewhere mentioned in the Bible, I think, that a serpent hatched out of a cock's egg –

Sylvester A cock's egg! It couldn't have been the egg of an ordinary cock. Not the male of what we call a hen?

Simon I think so.

Sylvester Well, be-God, that's a good one! You know Susie'll have to be told to disintensify her soul-huntin', for religion even isn't an excuse for saying that a man 'll become a cockatrice.

Simon In a church, somehow or other, it seems natural enough, and even in the street it's alright, for one thing is as good as another in the wide-open ear of the air, but in the delicate quietness of your own home it, it –

Sylvester Jars on you!

Simon Exactly!

Sylvester If she'd only confine her glory-to-God business to the festivals, Christmas, now, or even Easter, Simon, it would be recommendable; for a few days before Christmas, like the quiet raisin' of a curtain, an' a few days after, like the gentle lowerin' of one, there's nothing more . . . more –

Simon Appropriate . . .

Sylvester Exhilaratin' than the singin' of the Adestay Fidellis.

Simon She's damned pretty, an' if she dressed herself justly, she'd lift some man's heart up, an' toss down many another. It's a mystery now, what affliction causes the disablement, for most women of that kind are plain, an' when a woman's born plain she's born good. I wonder what caused the peculiar bend in Susie's nature? Narrow your imagination to the limit and you couldn't call it an avocation.

Sylvester (*giving the head of his pipe a sharp, quick blow on the palm of his hand to clear it*) Adoration.

Simon What?

Sylvester Adoration, Simon, accordin' to the flesh . . . She fancied Harry and Harry fancied Jessie, so she hides her rage an' loss in the love of a scorchin' Gospel.

Simon Strange, strange.

Sylvester Oh, very curious, Simon.

Simon It's a problem, I suppose.

Sylvester An inconsolable problem, Simon.

Mrs Foran enters by door, helping in Mrs Heegan, who is pale and shivering with cold.

Mrs Heegan (*shivering and shuddering*) U-u-uh, I feel the stream of blood that's still trickling through me old veins icifyin' fast; u-uh.

Mrs Foran Madwoman, dear, to be waitin' out there on the quay an' a wind risin' as cold as a stepmother's breath, piercin' through your old bones, mockin' any effort a body would make to keep warm, an' –

Suddenly she rushes over to the fireplace in an agony of dismay, scattering Simon and Sylvester, and whipping the frying pan off the fire.

The steak, the steak; I forgot the blasted steak an' onions fryin' on the fire! God Almighty, there's not as much as a bead of juice left in either of them. The scent of the burnin' would penetrate to the street, an' not one of you'd stir a hand to lift them out of danger. Oh, look at the condition they're in. Even the gospel-gunner couldn't do a little target practice by helpin' the necessity of a neighbour. (*As she goes out.*) I can hear the love for your neighbours almost fizzlin' in your hearts.

Mrs Heegan (*pushing in to the fire, to Simon and Sylvester*) Push to the right and push to the left till I get to the fosterin' fire. Time eatin' his heart out, an' no sign of him yet. The two of them, the two of my legs is numb . . . an' the wind's risin' that'll make the sea heave an' sink under the boat tonight, under shaded lights an' the submarines about.

Susie comes in, goes over to window, and looks out.

Hours ago the football match must have been over, an' no word of him yet, an' all drinkin' if they won, an' all drinkin' if they lost; with Jessie hitchin' on after him, an' no one thinkin' of me an' the maintenance money.

Sylvester He'll come back in time; he'll have to come back; he must come back.

Simon He got the goals, Mrs Heegan, that won the last two finals, and it's only fair he'd want to win this, which'll mean that the Cup won before two –

Sylvester (*butting in*) – times hand runnin' –

Simon – two times consecutively before, makin' the Cup the property of the Club.

Sylvester Exactly!

Mrs Heegan The chill's residin' in my bones, an' feelin's left me just the strength to shiver. He's overstayed his leave a lot, an' if he misses now the tide that's waitin', he skulks behind desertion from the colours.

Susie On Active Service that means death at dawn.

Mrs Heegan An' my governmental money grant would stop at once.

Susie That would gratify Miss Jessie Taite, because you put her weddin' off with Harry till after the duration of the war, an' cut her out of the allowance.

Sylvester (*with a sickened look at Simon*) Dtch, dtch, dtch, the way the women wag the worst things out of happenings! (*To the women.*) My God Almighty, he'll be back in time an' fill yous all with disappointment.

Mrs Heegan She's coinin' money workin' at munitions, an' doesn't need to eye the little that we get from Harry; for one evening hurryin' with him to the pictures she left her bag behind, an' goin' through it what would you think I found?

Susie A saucy book, now, or a naughty picture?

Mrs Heegan Lion and Unicorn standin' on their Jew ay mon draw. With all the rings an' dates, an' rules an' regulations.

Simon What was it, Mrs Heegan?

Mrs Heegan Spaced an' lined; signed an' signatured; nestlin' in a blue envelope to keep it warm.

Sylvester (*testily*) Oh, sing it out, woman, an' don't be takin' the value out of what you're goin' to tell us.

Mrs Heegan A Post Office Savings Bank Book.

Sylvester Oh, hairy enough, eh?

Simon How much, Mrs Heegan?

Mrs Heegan Pounds an' shillings with the pence missin'; backed by secrecy, an' security guaranteed by Act of Parliament.

Sylvester (*impatiently*) Dtch, dtch. Yes, yes, woman, but how much was it?

Mrs Heegan Two hundred an' nineteen pounds, sixteen shillings, an' no pence.

Sylvester Be God, a nice little nest egg, right enough!

Susie I hope in my heart that she came by it honestly, and that she remembers that it's as true now as when it was first spoken that it's harder for a camel to go through the eye of a needle than for a rich person to enter the kingdom of heaven.

Simon And she hidin' it all under a veil of silence, when there wasn't the slightest fear of any of us bein' jealous of her.

A tumult is heard on the floor over their heads, followed by a crash of breaking delft. They are startled, and listen attentively.

Mrs Heegan (*breaking the silence*) Oh, there he's at it again. An' she sayin' that he was a pattern husband since he came home on leave, merry-making with her an' singin' dolorously the first thing every mornin'. I was thinkin' there'd be a rough house sometime over her lookin' so well after his long absence . . . you'd imagine now, the trenches would have given him some idea of the sacredness of life!

Another crash of breaking delftware.

An' the last week of his leave she was too fond of breakin' into song in front of him.

Sylvester Well, she's gettin' it now for goin' round heavin' her happiness in the poor man's face.

A crash, followed by screams from Mrs Foran.

Susie I hope he won't be running down here as he often does.

Simon (*a little agitated*) I couldn't stay here an' listen to that; I'll go up and stop him: he might be killing the poor woman.

Mrs Heegan Don't do anything of the kind, Simon; he might down you with a hatchet or something.

Simon Phuh, I'll keep him off with the left and hook him with the right. (*Putting on his hat and coat as he goes to the door.*) Looking prim and careless 'll astonish him. Monstrous to stay here, while he may be killing the woman.

Mrs Heegan (*to Simon as he goes out*) For God's sake mind yourself, Simon.

Sylvester (*standing beside closed door on right with his ear close to one of the panels, listening intently*) Simon's a tidy little man with his fists, an' would make Teddy Foran feel giddy if he got home with his left hook.

Crash.

I wonder is that Simon knockin' down Foran, or Foran knockin' down Simon?

Mrs Heegan If he came down an' we had the light low, an' kept quiet, he might think we were all out.

Sylvester Shush. I can hear nothin' now. Simon must have awed him. Quiet little man, but when Simon gets goin' . . . Shush? No, nothin' . . . Something unusual has happened. O, oh, be-God!

The door against which Sylvester is leaning bursts in suddenly. Sylvester is flung headlong to the floor, and Mrs Foran, her hair falling wildly over her shoulders, a cut over her eye, frantic with fear, rushes in and scrambles in a frenzy of haste under the bed. Mrs Heegan, quickened by fear, runs like a good one, followed by Susie, into the room, the door of which

18

they bang after them. Sylvester hurriedly fights his way
under the bed with Mrs Foran.

Mrs Foran (*speaking excitedly and jerkily as she climbs
under the bed*) Flung his dinner into the fire – and started
to smash the little things in the room. Tryin' to save the
dresser, I got a box in the eye. I locked the door on him
as I rushed out, an' before I was halfway down, he had
one of the panels flyin' out with – a hatchet!

Sylvester (*under the bed – out of breath*) Why the hell
didn't you sing out before you sent the door flyin' in on
top o' me!

Mrs Foran How could I an' I flyin' before danger to me –
life?

Sylvester Yes, an' you've got me into a nice extremity
now!

Mrs Foran An' I yelled to Simon Norton when he had
me – down, but the boyo only ran the faster out of the –
house!

Sylvester Oh, an' the regal like way he went out to fight!
Oh, I'm findin' out that everyone who wears a cocked hat
isn't a Napoleon!

*Teddy Foran, Mrs Foran's husband, enters by door,
with a large, fancy, vividly yellow-coloured bowl,
ornamented with crimson roses, in one hand and a
hatchet in the other. He is big and powerful, rough and
hardy. A man who would be dominant in a public
house, and whose opinions would be listened to with
great respect. He is dressed in khaki uniform of a
soldier home on leave.*

Teddy Under the bed, eh! Right place for a guilty
conscience. I should have thrown you out of the window
with the dinner you put before me. Out with you from
under there, an' come up with your husband.

Susie (*opening suddenly door right, putting in her head, pulling it back and shutting door again*) God is looking at you, God is looking at you!

Mrs Foran I'll not budge an inch from where I am.

Teddy (*looking under the bed and seeing Sylvester*) What are you doin' there encouragin' her against her husband?

Sylvester You've no right to be rippin' open the poor woman's life of peace with violence.

Teddy (*with indignation*) She's my wife, isn't she?

Mrs Foran Nice thing if I lose the sight of my eye with the cut you gave me!

Teddy She's my wife, isn't she? An' you've no legal right to be harbourin' her here, keepin' her from her household duties. Stunned I was when I seen her lookin' so well after me long absence. Blowin' her sighin' in me face all day, an' she sufferin' the tortures of hell for fear I'd miss the boat!

Sylvester Go on up to your own home; you've no right to be violatin' this place.

Teddy You'd like to make her your cheery amee, would you? It's napoo, there, napoo, you little pipsqueak. I seen you an' her goin' down the street arm-in-arm.

Sylvester Did you expect to see me goin' down the street leg-in-leg with her?

Teddy Thinkin' of her ring-papers instead of her husband. (*To Mrs Foran,*) I'll teach you to be rippling with joy an' your husband goin' away!

He shows the bowl.

Your weddin' bowl, look at it; pretty, isn't it? Take your last eyeful of it now, for it's goin' west quick!

Susie (*popping her head in again*) God is watching you, God is watching you!

Mrs Foran (*appealingly*) Teddy, Teddy, don't smash the poor weddin' bowl.

Teddy (*smashing the bowl with a blow of the hatchet*) It would be a pity, wouldn't it? Damn it, an' damn you. I'm off now to smash anything I missed, so that you'll have a gay time fittin' up the little home again by the time your loving husband comes back. You can come an' have a look, an' bring your mon amee if you like.

He goes out, and there is a pause as Mrs Foran and Sylvester peep anxiously towards the door.

Sylvester Cautious, now, cautious; he might be lurking outside that door there, ready to spring on you the minute you show'd your nose!

Mrs Foran Me lovely little weddin' bowl, me lovely little weddin' bowl!

Teddy is heard breaking things in the room above.

Sylvester (*creeping out from under the bed*) Oh, he is gone up. He was a little cow'd, I think, when he saw me.

Mrs Foran Me little weddin' bowl, wrapp'd in tissue paper, an' only taken out for a few hours every Christmas – me poor little weddin' bowl.

Susie (*popping her head in*) God is watching – oh, he's gone!

Sylvester (*jubilant*) Vanished! He was a little cow'd, I think, when he saw me.

Mrs Heegan and Susie come into the room.

Mrs Foran He's makin' a hash of every little thing we have in the house, Mrs Heegan.

Mrs Heegan Go inside to the room, Mrs Foran, an' if he comes down again, we'll say you ran out to the street.

Mrs Foran (*going into room*) My poor little weddin' bowl that I might have had for generations!

Susie (*who has been looking out of the window, excitedly*) They're comin', they're comin': a crowd with a concertina; some of them carrying Harry on their shoulders, an' others are carrying that Jessie Taite too, holding a silver cup in her hands. Oh, look at the shameful way she's showing her legs to all who like to have a look at them!

Mrs Heegan Never mind Jessie's legs – what we have to do is to hurry him out in time to catch the boat.

The sound of a concertina playing in the street outside has been heard, and the noise of a marching crowd. The crowd stops at the house. Shouts are heard – 'Up the Avondales!'; 'Up Harry Heegan and the Avondales!' Then steps are heard coming up the stairs, and first Simon Norton enters, holding the door ceremoniously wide open to allow Harry to enter, with his arm around Jessie, who is carrying a silver cup joyously, rather than reverentially, elevated, as a priest would elevate a chalice.

Harry is wearing khaki trousers, a military cap stained with trench mud, a vivid orange-coloured jersey with black collar and cuffs. He is twenty-three years of age, tall, with the sinewy muscles of a manual worker made flexible by athletic sport. He is a typical young worker, enthusiastic, very often boisterous, sensible by instinct rather than by reason. He has gone to the trenches as unthinkingly as he would go to the polling booth. He isn't naturally stupid; it is the stupidity of persons in high places that has stupefied him. He has given all to his masters, strong heart, sound lungs, healthy stomach, lusty limbs and the little mind that education has permitted to develop sufficiently to make all the rest a little more useful He is excited now with the sweet and innocent insanity of a fine achievement, and the rapid lowering of a few drinks.

Jessie is twenty-two or so, responsive to all the animal impulses of life. Ever dancing around, in and between the world, the flesh, and the devil. She would be happy climbing with a boy among the heather on Howth Hill, and could play ball with young men on the swards of the Phoenix Park. She gives her favour to the prominent and popular. Harry is her favourite: his strength and speed has won the Final for his club, he wears the ribbon of the DCM. It is a time of spiritual and animal exaltation for her.

Barney Bagnal, a soldier mate of Harry's, stands a little shyly near the door, with a pleasant, good-humoured grin on his rather broad face. He is the same age as Harry, just as strong, but not so quick, less finely formed, and not so sensitive; able to take most things quietly, but savage and wild when he becomes enraged. He is fully dressed, with topcoat buttoned on him, and he carries Harry's on his arm.

Harry (*joyous and excited*) Won, won, won, be-God; by the odd goal in five. Lift it up, lift it up, Jessie, sign of youth, sign of strength, sign of victory!

Mrs Heegan (*to Sylvester*) I knew, now, Harry would come back in time to catch the boat.

Harry (*to Jessie*) Leave it here, leave it down here, Jessie, under the picture, the picture of the boy that won the final.

Mrs Heegan A parcel of sandwiches, a bottle of whiskey, an' some magazines to take away with you an' Barney, Harry.

Harry Napoo sandwiches, an' napoo magazines: look at the cup, eh? The cup that Harry won, won by the odd goal in five! (*To Barney.*) The song that the little Jock used to sing, Barney, what was it? The little Jock we left shrivellin' on the wire after the last push.

Barney 'Will ye no come back again'?

Harry No, no, the one we all used to sing with him, 'The Silver Tassie'. (*Pointing to cup*) There it is, the Silver Tassie, won by the odd goal in five, kicked by Harry Heegan.

Mrs Heegan Watch your time, Harry, watch your time.

Jessie He's watching it, he's watching it – for God's sake don't get fussy, Mrs Heegan.

Harry They couldn't take their beatin' like men . . . Play the game, play the game, why the hell couldn't they play the game? (*To Barney.*) See the President of the Club, Dr Forby Maxwell, shaking hands with me, when he was giving me the cup, 'Well done, Heegan!' The way they yell'd and jump'd when they put in the equalising goal in the first half!

Barney Ay, a fluke, that's what it was; a lousy fluke.

Mrs Heegan (*holding Harry's coat up for him to put it on*) Here, your coat, Harry, slip it on while you're talkin'.

Harry (*putting it on*) Alright, keep smiling, don't fuss. (*To the rest,*) Grousing the whole time they were chasing the ball; an' when they lost it, 'Referee, referee, offside, referee . . . Foul there; eh, open your eyes, referee!'

Jessie And we scream'd and shout'd them down with 'Play the game, Primrose Rovers, play the game!'

Barney You ran them off their feet till they nearly stood still.

Mrs Foran has been peeping in twice timidly from the room and now comes in to the rest.

Mrs Foran Somebody run up an' bring Teddy down for fear he'd be left behind.

Sylvester (*to Harry*) Your haversack an' trench tools, Harry; haversack first, isn't it?

Harry (*fixing his haversack*) Haversack, haversack, don't rush me. (*To the rest.*) But when I got the ball, Barney, once I got the ball, the rain began to fall on the others. An' the last goal, the goal that put us one ahead, the winning goal, that was a-a-eh-a stunner!

Barney A beauty, me boy, a hot beauty.

Harry Slipping by the back rushing at me like a mad bull, steadying a moment for a drive, seeing in a flash the goalie's hands sent with a shock to his chest by the force of the shot, his half-stunned motion to clear, a charge, and then carrying him, the ball and all with a rush into the centre of the net!

Barney (*enthusiastically*) Be-God, I did get a thrill when I seen you puttin' him sittin' on his arse in the middle of the net!

Mrs Foran (*from the door*) One of yous do go up an' see if Teddy's ready to go.

Mrs Heegan (*to Harry*) Your father'll carry your kitbag, an' Jessie 'll carry your rifle as far as the boat.

Harry (*irritably*) Oh, damn it, woman, give your wailin' over for a minute!

Mrs Heegan You've got only a few bare minutes to spare, Harry.

Harry We'll make the most of them, then. (*To Barney.*) Out with one of them wine-virgins we got in 'The Mill in the Field', Barney, and we'll rape her in a last hot moment before we set out to kiss the guns!

Simon has gone into room and returned with a gun and a kitbag. He crosses to where Barney is standing.

Barney (*taking a bottle of wine from his pocket*) Empty her of her virtues, eh?

Harry Spill it out, Barney, spill it out . . .

He seizes the silver cup, and holds it towards Barney.

Here, into the cup, be-God. A drink out of the cup, out of the Silver Tassie!

Barney (*who has removed the cap and taken out the cork*) Here she is now . . . Ready for anything, stripp'd to the skin!

Jessie No double-meaning talk, Barney.

Susie (*haughtily, to Jessie*) The men that are defending us have leave to bow themselves down in the House of Rimmon, for the men that go with the guns are going with God.

Barney pours wine into the cup for Harry and into a glass for himself.

Harry (*to Jessie*) Jessie, a sup for you.

Jessie drinks from the cup.

An' a drink for me. (*He drinks.*) Now a kiss while our lips are wet. (*He kisses her.*) Christ, Barney, how would you like to be retreating from the fairest face and – (*lifting Jessie's skirt a little*) and the trimmest, slimmest little leg in the parish? Napoo, Barney, to everyone but me!

Mrs Foran One of you go up, an' try to get my Teddy down.

Barney (*lifting Susie's skirt a little*) Napoo, Harry, to everyone but –

26

Susie (*angrily, pushing Barney away from her*) You khaki-cover'd ape, you, what are you trying to do? Manhandle the lassies of France, if you like, but put on your gloves when you touch a woman that seeketh not the things of the flesh.

Harry (*putting an arm round Susie to mollify her*) Now, Susie, Susie, lengthen your temper for a passing moment, so that we may bring away with us the breath of a kiss to the shell-bullied air of the trenches . . . Besides, there's nothing to be ashamed of – it's not a bad little leggie at all.

Susie (*slipping her arm round Harry's neck, and looking defiantly at Barney*) I don't mind what Harry does; I know he means no harm, not like other people. Harry's different.

Jessie You'll not forget to send me the German helmet home from France, Harry?

Susie (*trying to rest her head on Harry's breast*) I know Harry, he's different. It's his way. I wouldn't let anyone else touch me, but in some way or another I can tell Harry's different.

Jessie (*putting her arm round Harry under Susie's in an effort to dislodge it*) Susie, Harry wants to be free to keep his arm round me during his last few moments here, so don't be pulling him about!

Susie (*shrinking back a little*) I was only saying that Harry was different.

Mrs Foran For God's sake, will someone go up for Teddy, or he won't go back at all!

Teddy (*appearing at door*) Damn anxious for Teddy to go back! Well, Teddy's goin' back, an' he's left everything tidy upstairs so that you'll not have much trouble sortin' things out. (*To Harry*) The Club an' a crowd's waitin' outside to bring us to the boat before they go to the spread in honour of the final. (*Bitterly.*) A party for them while we muck off to the trenches!

Harry (*after a slight pause, to Barney*) Are you game, Barney?

Barney What for?

Harry To go to the spread and hang the latch for another night?

Barney (*taking his rifle from Simon and slinging it over his shoulder*) No, no, napoo desertin' on Active Service. Deprivation of pay an' the rest of your time in the front trenches. No, no. We must go back!

Mrs Heegan No, no, Harry. You must go back.

Simon
Sylvester } (*together*) You must go back.
Susie

Voices of Crowd Outside They must go back!

The ship's siren is heard blowing.

Simon The warning signal.

Sylvester By the time they get there, they'll be unslinging the gangways!

Susie (*handing Harry his steel helmet*) Here's your helmet, Harry.

He puts it on.

Mrs Heegan You'll all nearly have to run for it now!

Sylvester I've got your kitbag, Harry.

Susie I've got your rifle.

Simon I'll march in front with the cup, after Conroy with the concertina.

Teddy Come on: ong, avong to the trenches!

Harry (*recklessly*) Jesus, a last drink, then!

He raises the silver cup. Singing:

Gae bring to me a pint of wine,
And fill it in a silver tassie;

Barney (*joining in vigorously*)
. . . a silver tassie.

Harry
That I may drink before I go,
A service to my bonnie lassie.

Barney
. . . bonnie lassie.

Harry
The boat rocks at the pier o' Leith,
Full loud the wind blows from the ferry;
The ship rides at the Berwick Law,
An' I must leave my bonnie Mary!

Barney
. . . leave my bonnie Mary!

Harry
The trumpets sound, the banners fly,
The glittering spears are ranked ready;

Barney
. . . glittering spears are ranked ready;

Harry
The shouts of war are heard afar,
The battle closes thick and bloody.

Barney
. . . closes thick and bloody.

Harry
It's not the roar of sea or shore,
That makes me longer wish to tarry,
Nor shouts of war that's heard afar –
It's leaving thee, my bonnie lassie!

Barney
. . . leaving thee, my bonnie lassie!

Teddy Come on, come on.

Simon, Sylvester and Susie go out.

Voices (*outside*)
Come on from your home to the boat;
Carry on from the boat to the camp.

Teddy and Barney go out. Harry and Jessie follow; as Harry reaches the door, he takes his arm from round Jessie and comes back to Mrs Heegan.

Voices (*outside*)
From the camp up to the lines to the trenches.

Harry (*shyly and hurriedly kissing Mrs Heegan*) Well, goodbye, old woman.

Mrs Heegan Goodbye, my son.

Harry goes out. The chorus of 'The Silver Tassie', accompanied by a concertina, can be heard growing fainter till it ceases. Mrs Foran goes out timidly. Mrs Heegan pokes the fire, arranges the things in the room, and then goes to the window and looks out. After a pause, the loud and long blast of the ship's siren is heard. The light on the masthead, seen through the window, moves slowly away, and Mrs Heegan with a sigh, 'Ah dear', goes over to the fire and sits down. A slight pause, then Mrs Foran returns to the room.

Mrs Foran Every little bit of china I had in the house is lyin' above in a mad an' muddled heap like the flotsum an' jetsum of the seashore!

Mrs Heegan (*with a deep sigh of satisfaction*) Thanks be to Christ that we're after managin' to get the three of them away safely.

End of Act One.

Act Two

*In the war zone: a scene of jagged and lacerated ruin of
what was once a monastery. At back a lost wall and
window are indicated by an arched piece of broken
coping pointing from the left to the right, and a similar
piece of masonry pointing from the right to the left.
Between these two lacerated fingers of stone can be seen
the country stretching to the horizon where the front
trenches are. Here and there heaps of rubbish mark
where houses once stood. From some of these, lean, dead
hands are protruding. Further on, spiky stumps of trees
which were once a small wood. The ground is dotted
with rayed and shattered shell holes. Across the horizon
in the red glare can be seen the criss-cross pattern of the
barbed wire bordering the trenches. In the sky sometimes
a green star, sometimes a white star, burns.*

*Within the broken archway to the left is an arched
entrance to another part of the monastery, used now as a
Red Cross Station. In the wall, right, near the front is a
stained-glass window, background green, figure of the
Virgin, white-faced, wearing a black robe, lights inside
making the figure vividly apparent. Further up from this
window is a life-size crucifix. A shell has released an arm
from the cross, which has caused the upper part of the
figure to lean forward with the released arm outstretched
towards the figure of the Virgin. Underneath the crucifix
on a pedestal, in red letters, are the words:* PRINCEPS
PACIS. *Almost opposite the crucifix is a gunwheel to which
Barney is tied.*

*At the back, in the centre, where the span of the arch
should be, is the shape of a big howitzer gun, squat,*

*heavy underpart, with a long, sinister barrel now pointing
towards the front at an angle of forty-five degrees. At the
base of the gun a piece of wood is placed on which is
chalked,* HYDE PARK CORNER. *On another piece of
wood near the entrance of the Red Cross Station is
chalked* NO HAWKERS OR STREET CRIES PERMITTED
HERE. *In the near centre is a brazier in which a fire is
burning. Crouching above, on a ramp, is a soldier whose
clothes are covered with mud and splashed with blood.*

*Every feature of the scene seems a little distorted from
its original appearance. Rain is falling steadily; its fall
worried now and again by fitful gusts of a cold wind.
A small organ is heard playing slow and stately notes as
the curtain rises.*

*After a pause, the Croucher, without moving, intones
dreamily:*

Croucher
And the hand of the Lord was upon me, and carried
me out in the spirit of the Lord, and set me down
in the midst of a valley.
And I looked and saw a great multitude that stood
upon their feet, an exceeding great army.
And he said unto me, Son of man, can this exceeding
great army become a valley of dry bones?

*The music ceases, and a voice, in the part of the
monastery left standing, intones: 'Kyr . . . ie . . . e . . .
eleison. Kyr . . . ie . . . e . . . eleison,' followed by the
answer: 'Christe . . . eleison.'*

(*Resuming.*) And I answered, O Lord God, thou knowest.
And he said, prophesy and say unto the wind, come
from the four winds a breath and breathe upon these
living that they may die.

*As he pauses the voice in the monastery is heard again:
'Gloria in excelsis Deo et in terra pax hominibus
bonae voluntatis.'*

(*Resuming.*) And I prophesied, and the breath came out of them, and the sinews came away from them, and behold a shaking, and their bones fell asunder, bone from his bone, and they died, and the exceeding great army became a valley of dry bones.

The voice from the monastery is heard, clearly for the first half of the sentence, then dying away towards the end: 'Accendat in nobis Dominus ignem sui amor is, et flammam aeternae caritatis.'

A group of soldiers comes in from fatigue, bunched together as if for comfort and warmth. They are wet and cold, and they are sullen-faced. They form a circle around the brazier and stretch their hands towards the blaze.

First Soldier Cold and wet and tir'd.

Second Soldier Wet and tir'd and cold.

Third Soldier Tir'd and cold and wet.

Fourth Soldier (*very like Teddy*) Twelve blasted hours of ammunition transport fatigue!

First Soldier Twelve weary hours.

Second Soldier And wasting hours.

Third Soldier And hot and heavy hours.

First Soldier Toiling and thinking to build the wall of force that blocks the way from here to home.

Second Soldier Lifting shells.

Third Soldier Carrying shells.

Fourth Soldier Piling shells.

First Soldier In the falling, pissing rine and whistling wind.

Second Soldier The whistling wind and falling, drenching rain.

Third Soldier The God-damn rain and blasted whistling wind.

First Soldier And the shirkers sife at home coil'd up at ease.

Second Soldier Shells for us and pianos for them.

Third Soldier Fur coats for them and winding-sheets for us.

Fourth Soldier Warm.

Second Soldier And dry.

First Soldier An' 'appy.

A slight pause.

Barney An' they call it re-cu-per-at-ing!

First Soldier (*reclining near the fire*) Gawd, I'm sleepy.

Second Soldier (*reclining*) Tir'd and lousey.

Third Soldier (*reclining*) Damp and shaking.

Fourth Soldier (*murmuringly, the rest joining him*) Tir'd and lousey an' wet an' sleepy, but mother call me early in the morning.

First Soldier (*dreamily*) Wen I thinks of 'ome, I thinks of a field of dysies.

The Rest (*dreamily*) Wen 'e thinks of 'ome, 'e thinks of a field of dysies.

First Soldier (*chanting dreamily*)
  I sees the missus paryding along Walham Green,
  Through the jewels an' silks on the costers' carts,
  Emmie a-pulling her skirt an' muttering,

'A balloon, a balloon, I wants a balloon',
The missus a-tugging 'er on, an' sying,
'A balloon, for shime, an' your father fighting:
You'll wait till 'e's 'ome, an' the bands a-plying!'

He pauses.

(*Suddenly.*) But wy'r we 'ere, wy'r we 'ere – that's wot we wants to know!

Second Soldier God only knows – or else, perhaps, a red-cap.

First Soldier (*chanting*)
Tabs'll murmur, 'em an' 'aw, an' sy: 'You're 'ere because you're
Point nine double-o, the sixth platoon an' forty-eight battalion,
The Yellow Plumes that pull'd a bow at Crecy,
And gave to fame a leg up on the path to glory;
Now with the howitzers of the Twenty-first Division,
Tiking life easy with the Army of the Marne,
An' all the time the battered Conchie squeals,
"It's one or two men looking after business".'

Third Soldier An' saves his blasted skin!

First Soldier (*chanting*) The padre gives a fag an' softly whispers:

'Your king, your country an' your muvver 'as you 'ere.'
An' last time 'ome on leave, I awsks the missus:
'The good God up in heaven, Bill, 'e knows,
An' I gets the seperytion moneys reg'lar.'

He sits up suddenly.

But wy'r we 'ere, wy'r we 'ere – that's wot I wants to know?

The Rest (*chanting sleepily*) Why's 'e 'ere, why's 'e 'ere – that's wot 'e wants to know!

Barney (*singing to the air of second bar in chorus of 'Auld Lang Syne'*) We're here because we're here, because we're here, because we're here!

Each slides into an attitude of sleep – even Barney's head droops a little. The Corporal, followed by the Visitor, appears at back. The Visitor is a portly man with a rubicund face; he is smiling to demonstrate his ease of mind, but the lines are a little distorted with an ever-present sense of anxiety. He is dressed in a semi-civilian, semi-military manner – dark worsted suit, shrapnel helmet, a haversack slung round his shoulder, a brown belt round his middle, black top boots and spurs, and he carries a cane. His head is bent between his shoulders, and his shoulders are crouched a little.

Visitor Yes, tomorrow, I go a little further. Penetrate a little deeper into danger. Foolish, yes, but then it's an experience; by God, it's an experience. The military authorities are damned strict – won't let a . . . man . . . plunge!

Corporal In a manner of speakin', sir, only let you see the arses of the guns.

Visitor (*not liking the remark*) Yes, no; no, oh yes. Damned strict, won't let a . . . man . . . plunge! (*Suddenly, with alarm.*) What's that, what was that?

Corporal Wha' was what?

Visitor A buzz, I thought I heard a buzz.

Corporal A buzz?

Visitor Of an aeroplane.

Corporal Didn't hear. Might have been a bee.

Visitor No, no; don't think it was a bee. (*Arranging helmet with his hands.*) Damn shrapnel helmet; skin tight; like a vice; hurts the head. Rather be without it;

37

but, regulations, you know. Military authorities damn particular – won't let a . . . man . . . plunge! (*Seeing Barney.*) Aha, what have we got here, what have we got here?

Corporal (*to Barney*) 'Tshun! (*To the Visitor.*) Regimental misdemeanour, sir.

Visitor (*to Barney*) Nothing much, boy, nothing much?

Barney (*chanting softly*)
A brass-hat pullin' the bedroom curtains
Between himself, the world an' the estaminay's daughter,
In a pyjama'd hurry ran down an' phon'd
A Tommy was chokin' an estaminay cock,
An' I was pinch'd as I was puttin' the bird
Into a pot with a pint of peas.

Corporal (*chanting hoarsely*)
And the hens all droop, for the loss has made
The place a place of desolation!

Visitor (*reprovingly, to the Corporal*) Seriously, Corporal, seriously, please. Sacred, sacred: property of the citizen of a friendly State, sacred. On Active Service, serious to steal a fowl, a cock. (*To Barney.*) The uniform, the cause, boy, the corps. Infra dignitatem, boy, infra dignitatem.

Barney Wee, wee.

Visitor (*pointing to reclining soldiers*) Taking it easy, eh?

Corporal Done in; transport fatigue; twelve hours.

Visitor Um, not too much rest, Corporal. Dangerous. Keep 'em moving much as possible. Too much rest – bad. Sap, sap, sap.

Corporal (*pointing to the left*) Bit of monastery left intact. Hold services there; troops off to front line. Little organ plays.

Visitor Splendid. Bucks 'em up. Gives 'em peace.

A Staff Officer enters suddenly, passing by the Visitor with a springing hop, so that he stands in the centre with the Visitor on his right and the Corporal on his left. He is prim, pert, and polished, superfine khaki uniform, gold braid, crimson tabs, and gleaming top boots. He speaks his sentences with a gasping importance.

Corporal (*stiffening*) 'Shun! Staff!

The Soldiers spring to their feet. The Croucher remains as he is, with a sleepy alertness.

Soldiers Staff! 'Shun!

Corporal (*bellowing at the Croucher*) Eh, you there: 'shun! Staff!

Croucher (*calmly*) Not able. Sick. Privilege. Excused duty.

Staff-Wallah (*reading document*)
Battery Brigade Orders, F.A., 31 D 2.
Units presently recuperating, parade eight o'clock p.m.
Attend Lecture organised by Society for Amusement
    and Mental Development, Soldiers at Front.
Subject: Habits of those living between Frigid Zone
    and Arctic Circle.
Lecturer: Mr Melville Sprucer.
Supplementary Order: Units to wear gas masks.
As you were.

The Staff-Wallah departs as he came with a springing hop. The Visitor and the Corporal relax, and stroll down towards the RC Station. The soldiers relax too, seeking various positions of ease around the fire.

Visitor (*indicating RC Station*) Ah, in here. We'll just pop in here for a minute. And then pop out again.

He and the Corporal go into the RC Station. A pause.

First Soldier (*chanting and indicating that he means the Visitor by looking in the direction of the RC Station*)
The perky bastard's cautious nibbling
In a safe, safe shelter at danger queers me.
Furiously feeling he's up to the neck in
The whirl and the sweep of the front-line fighting.

Second Soldier (*chanting*)
In his full-blown, chin-strapp'd, shrapnel helmet,
He'll pat a mug on the back and murmur,
'Here's a stand-fast Tauntonshire before me',
And the mug, on his feet, 'll whisper 'yessir'.

Third Soldier (*chanting*)
Like a bride, full-flush'd, 'e'll sit down and listen
To every word of the goddam sermon,
From the cushy-soul'd, word-spreading, yellow-streaked
dud.

Barney (*chanting*)
Who wouldn't make a patch on a Tommy's backside.

A pause.

First Soldier 'Ow long have we been resting 'ere?

Second Soldier A month.

Third Soldier Twenty-nine days, twenty-three hours and – (*looking at watch*) twenty-three minutes.

Fourth Soldier Thirty-seven minutes more'll make it thirty days.

Croucher
Thirty days hath September, April, June, and November
November – that's the month when I was born –
November
Not the beginning, not the end, but the middle of
November.

Near the valley of the Thames, in the middle of
    November.
Shall I die at the start, near the end, in the middle of
    November?

First Soldier (*nodding towards the Croucher*) One more
scrap, an' 'e'll be Ay One in the kingdom of the bawmy.

Second Soldier Perhaps they have forgotten.

Third Soldier Forgotten.

Fourth Soldier Forgotten us.

First Soldier If the blighters at the front would tame their
grousing.

The Rest Tame their grousing.

Second Soldier And the wounded cease to stare their
silent scorning.

The Rest Passing by us, carried cushy on the stretchers.

Third Soldier We have beaten out the time upon the
duck-board.

Fourth Soldier Stiff standing watch'd the sunrise from
the firestep.

Second Soldier Stiff standing from the firestep watch'd
the sunset.

Third Soldier Have bless'd the dark wiring of the top
with curses.

Second Soldier And never a ray of leave.

Third Soldier To have a quiet drunk.

First Soldier Or a mad mowment to rustle a judy.

*Third Soldier takes out a package of cigarettes; taking
one himself he hands the package round. Each takes*

41

one, and the man nearest to Barney, kneeling up, puts one in his mouth and lights it for him. They all smoke silently for a few moments, sitting up round the fire.

Second Soldier (*chanting very earnestly and quietly*)
    Would God I smok'd an' walk'd an' watch'd th'
    Dance of a golden Brimstone butterfly,
    To the saucy pipe of a greenfinch resting
    In a drowsy, brambled lane in Cumberland.

First Soldier
    Would God I smok'd and lifted cargoes
    From the laden shoulders of London's river-way;
    Then holiday'd, roaring out courage and movement
    To the muscled machines of Tottenham Hotspur.

Third Soldier
    To hang here even a little longer,
    Lounging through fear-swell'd, anxious moments;
    The hinderparts of the god of battles
    Shading our war-tir'd eyes from his flaming face.

Barney
    If you creep to rest in a clos'd-up coffin,
    A tail of comrades seeing you safe home;
    Or be a kernel lost in a shell exploding –
    It's all, sure, only in a lifetime.

All (*together*)
    Each sparrow, hopping, irresponsible,
    Is indentur'd in God's mighty memory;
    And we, more than they all, shall not be lost
    In the forgetfulness of the Lord of Hosts.

The Visitor and the Corporal come from the Red Cross Station.

Visitor (*taking out a cigarette case*) Nurses too gloomy. Surgeons too serious. Doesn't do.

Corporal All lying-down cases, sir. Pretty bad.

Visitor (*who is now standing near the crucifix*) All the more reason make things merry and bright. Lift them out of themselves. (*To the Soldiers.*) See you all tomorrow at lecture?

First Soldier (*rising and standing a little sheepishly before the Visitor*) Yessir, yessir.

The Rest Yessir, yessir.

Visitor Good. Make it interesting. (*Searching in pocket.*) Damn it, have I none? Ah, saved.

He takes a match from his pocket and is about to strike it carelessly on the arm of the crucifix, when the First Soldier, with a rapid frightened movement, knocks it out of his hand.

First Soldier (*roughly*) Blarst you, man, keep your peace-white paws from that!

Second Soldier The image of the Son of God.

Third Soldier Jesus of Nazareth, the King of the Jews.

First Soldier (*reclining by the fire again*) There's a Gawd knocking abaht somewhere.

Fourth Soldier Wants Him to be sending us over a chit in the shape of a bursting shell.

Visitor Sorry put it across you. (*To Corporal.*) Too much time to think. Nervy. Time to brood, brood; bad. Sap. Sap. Sap. (*Walking towards where he came in.*) Must return quarters; rough and ready. Must stick it. There's a war on. Cheerio. Straight down road instead of round hill: shorter?

Corporal Less than half as long.

Visitor Safe?

43

Corporal Yes. Only drop shells off and on, crossroads. Ration party wip'd out week ago.

Visitor Go round hill. No hurry. General Officer's orders, no unnecessary risks. Must obey. Military Authorities damned particular – won't let a . . . man . . . plunge!

He and the Corporal go off. The soldiers in various attitudes are asleep around the fire. After a few moments' pause, two Stretcher-Bearers come in slowly from left, carrying a casualty. They pass through the sleeping soldiers, going towards the Red Cross Station. As they go they chant a verse, and as the verse is ending, they are followed by another pair carrying a second casualty.

First Bearers (*chanting*)
Oh, bear it gently, carry it softly –
A bullet or a shell said stop, stop, stop.
It's had its day, and it's left the play,
Since it gamboll'd over the top, top, top.
It's had its day and it's left the play,
Since it gamboll'd over the top.

Second Bearers (*chanting*)
Oh, carry it softly, bear it gently –
The beggar has seen it through, through, through.
If it 'adn't been 'im, if it 'adn't been 'im,
It might 'ave been me or you, you, you.
If it 'adn't been 'im, if it 'adn't been 'im,
It might 'ave been me or you.

Voice (*inside RC Station*) Easy, easy there; don't crowd.

First Stretcher-Bearer (*to man behind*) Whoa, whoa there, Bill, 'ouse full.

First Stretcher-Bearer (*behind, to those following*) Whoa, whoa; traffic blocked.

They leave the stretchers on the ground.

Wounded on the Stretchers (*chanting*)
    Carry on, carry on to the place of pain,
    Where the surgeon spreads his aid, aid, aid.
    And we show man's wonderful work, well done,
    To the image God hath made, made, made,
    And we show man's wonderful work, well done,
    To the image God hath made!

    When the future hours have all been spent,
    And the hand of death is near, near, near,
    Then a few, few moments and we shall find
    There'll be nothing left to fear, fear, fear,
    Then a few, few moments and we shall find
    There'll be nothing left to fear.

    The power, the joy, the pull of life,
    The laugh, the blow, and the dear kiss,
    The pride and hope, the gain and loss,
    Have been temper'd down to this, this, this,
    The pride and hope, the gain and loss,
    Have been temper'd down to this.

First Stretcher-Bearer (*to Barney*) Oh, Barney, have they
liced you up because you've kiss'd the Colonel's judy?

Barney They lit on me stealin' estaminay poulthry.

First Stretcher-Bearer A hen?

Second Stretcher-Bearer A duck, again, Barney?

Third Stretcher-Bearer A swan this time.

Barney (*chanting softly*)
    A Brass-hat pullin' the bedroom curtains
    Between himself, the world an' the estaminay's daughter,
    In a pyjama'd hurry ran down and phon'd
    A Tommy was chokin' an estaminay cock;
    An' I was pinch'd as I was puttin' the bird
    Into a pot with a pint of peas.

First Stretcher-Bearer The red-tabb'd squit!

Second Stretcher-Bearer The lousey map-scanner!

Third Stretcher-Bearer We must keep up, we must keep up the morale of the awmy.

Second Stretcher-Bearer (*loudly*) Does 'e eat well?

The Rest (*in chorus*) Yes, 'e eats well!

Second Stretcher-Bearer Does 'e sleep well?

The Rest (*in chorus*) Yes, 'e sleeps well!

Second Stretcher-Bearer Does 'e whore well?

The Rest (*in chorus*) Yes, 'e whores well!

Second Stretcher-Bearer Does 'e fight well?

The Rest (*in chorus*) Napoo; 'e 'as to do the thinking for the Tommies!

Voice (*from the RC Station*) Stretcher Party – carry on!

The Bearers stoop with precision, attach their supports to the stretchers, lift them up and march slowly into the RC Station, chanting.

Stretcher-Bearers (*chanting*)
Carry on – we've one bugled reason why –
We've 'eard and answer'd the call, call, call.
There's no more to be said, for when we are dead,
We may understand it all, all, all.
There's no more to be said, for when we are dead,
We may understand it all.

They go out, leaving the scene occupied by the Croucher and the Soldiers sleeping around the fire. The Corporal re-enters. He is carrying two parcels. He pauses, looking at the sleeping soldiers for a few moments, then shouts.

46

Corporal (*shouting*) Hallo, there, you sleepy blighters!
Number 2, a parcel; and for you, Number 3. Get a move
on – parcels!

The Soldiers wake up and spring to their feet.

For you, Number 2.

He throws a parcel to Second Soldier.

Number 3.

He throws the other parcel to Third Soldier.

Third Soldier (*taking paper from around his parcel*)
Looks like a bundle of cigarettes.

First Soldier Or a pack of cawds.

Fourth Soldier Or a prayer book.

Third Soldier (*astounded*) Holy Christ, it is!

The Rest What?

Third Soldier A prayer book!

Fourth Soldier In a green plush cover with a golden
cross.

Croucher Open it at the Psalms and sing that we may be
saved from the life and death of the beasts that perish.

Barney *Per omnia saecula saeculorum.*

Second Soldier (*who has opened his parcel*) A ball, be
God!

Fourth Soldier A red and yellow coloured rubber ball.

First Soldier And a note.

Second Soldier (*reading*) 'To play your way to the
enemies' trenches when you all go over the top. Mollie.'

First Soldier See if it 'ops.

*The Second Soldier hops the ball, and then kicks it
from him. The Corporal intercepts it, and begins to
dribble it across the stage. The Third Soldier tries to
take it from him. The Corporal shouts 'Offside, there!'
They play for a few minutes with the ball, when
suddenly the Staff-Wallah springs in and stands rigidly
in centre.*

Corporal (*stiff to attention as he sees the Staff-Wallah*)
'Shun. Staff!

*All the Soldiers stiffen. The Croucher remains
motionless.*

Corporal (*shouting to the Croucher*) You: 'shun. Staff!

Croucher Not able. Sick. Excused duty.

Staff-Wallah (*reading document*)
Brigade Orders, C/X 143. B/Y 341. Regarding gas
masks. Gas masks to be worn round neck so as to lie
in front 2½ degrees from socket of left shoulder-blade,
and 2¾ degrees from socket of right shoulder-blade,
leaving bottom margin to reach ¼ of an inch from
second button of lower end of tunic. Order to take
effect from 6 a.m. following morning of date received.
Dismiss!

He hops out again, followed by the Corporal.

First Soldier (*derisively*) Comprenneemoy.

Third Soldier Tray bong.

Second Soldier (*who is standing in archway, back,
looking scornfully after the Staff-Wallah, chanting*)
Jazzing back to his hotel he now goes gaily,
Shelter'd and safe where the clock ticks tamely.
His backside warming a cushion, downfill'd,
Green-clad, well splash'd with gold birds redbeak'd.

First Soldier

His last dim view of the front line sinking
Into the white-flesh'd breasts of a judy;
Cuddling with proud, bright, amorous glances
The thing salved safe from the mud of the trenches.

Second Soldier

His tunic reared in the lap of comfort,
Peeps at the blood-stain'd jackets passing,
Through colour-gay bars of ribbon jaunty,
Fresh from a posh shop snug in Bond Street.

Croucher

Shame and scorn play with and beat them,
Till we anchor in their company;
Then the decorations of security
Become the symbols of self-sacrifice.

A pause.

Second Soldier

A warning this that we'll soon be exiles
From the freedom chance of life can give,
To the front where you wait to be hurried breathless,
Murmuring how, how do you do, to God.

Third Soldier

Where hot with the sweat of mad endeavour,
Crouching to scrape a toy-deep shelter,
Quick-tim'd by hell's fast, frenzied drumfire
Exploding in flaming death around us.

Second Soldier

God, unchanging, heart-sicken'd, shuddering,
Gathereth the darkness of the night sky
To mask His paling countenance from
The blood dance of His self-slaying children.

Third Soldier

Stumbling, swiftly cursing, plodding,
Lumbering, loitering, stumbling, grousing,

Through mud and rain, and filth and danger,
Flesh and blood seek slow the front line.

Second Soldier
Squeals of hidden laughter run through
The screaming medley of the wounded –
Christ, who bore the cross, still weary,
Now trails a rope tied to a field gun.

*As the last notes of the chanting are heard the
Corporal comes in rapidly; he is excited but steady;
pale-faced and grim.*

Corporal They attack. Along a wide front the enemy
attacks. If they break through it may reach us even here.

Soldiers (*in chorus as they all put on gas masks*) They
attack. The enemy attacks.

Corporal Let us honour that in which we do put our trust.

Soldiers (*in chorus*) That it may not fail us in our time
of need.

*The Corporal goes over to the gun and faces towards
it, standing on the bottom step. The soldiers group
around, each falling upon one knee, their forms
crouched in a huddled act of obeisance. They are all
facing the gun with their backs to the audience. The
Croucher rises and joins them.*

Corporal (*singing*)
Hail cool-hardened tower of steel emboss'd
With the fever'd, figment thoughts of man;
Guardian of our love and hate and fear,
Speak for us to the inner ear of God!

Soldiers We believe in God and we believe in thee.

Corporal
Dreams of line, of colour, and of form;
Dreams of music dead for ever now;

Dreams in bronze and dreams in stone have gone
To make thee delicate and strong to kill.

Soldiers

We believe in God and we believe in thee.

Corporal

Jail'd in thy steel are hours of merriment
Cadg'd from the pageant-dream of children's play;
Too soon of the motley stripp'd that they may sweat
With them that toil for the glory of thy kingdom.

Soldiers We believe in God and we believe in thee.

Corporal

Remember our women, sad-hearted, proud-fac'd,
Who've given the substance of their womb for shadows;
Their shrivel'd, empty breasts war-tinselled
For patient gifts of graves to thee.

Soldiers We believe in God and we believe in thee.

Corporal

Dapple those who are shelter'd with disease,
And women labouring with child,
And children that play about the streets,
With blood of youth expiring in its prime.

Soldiers

We believe in God and we believe in thee.

Corporal

Tear a gap through the soul of our mass'd enemies;
Grant them all the peace of death;
Blow them swiftly into Abram's bosom,
And mingle them with the joys of paradise!

Soldiers

For we believe in God and we believe in thee.

*The sky has become vexed with a crimson glare, mixed
with yellow streaks, and striped with pillars of rising*

brown and black smoke. The Staff-Wallah rushes in,
turbulent and wild, with his uniform disordered.

Staff-Wallah

The enemy has broken through, broken through,
broken through!
Every man born of woman to the guns, to the guns.

Soldiers

To the guns, to the guns, to the guns!

Staff-Wallah

Those at prayer, all in bed, and the swillers drinking
deeply in the pubs.

Soldiers To the guns, to the guns.

Staff-Wallah

All the batmen, every cook, every bitch's son that hides
A whiff of courage in his veins,
Shelter'd vigour in his body,
That can run, or can walk, even crawl –
Dig him out, dig him out, shove him on –

Soldiers To the guns!

The Soldiers hurry to their places led by the Staff-
Wallah to the gun. The gun swings around and points
to the horizon; a shell is swung into the breech and a
flash indicates the firing of the gun; searchlights move
over the red glare of the sky; the scene darkens,
stabbed with distant flashes and by the more vivid
flash of the gun which the Soldiers load and fire with
rhythmical movements while the scene is closing. Only
flashes are seen; no noise is heard.

End of Act Two.

Act Three

The upper end of a hospital ward. At right angles from
back wall are two beds, one covered with a red quilt and
the other with a white one. From the centre of the head
of each bed is an upright having at the top a piece like a
swan's neck, curving out over the bed, from which hangs
a chain with a wooden cross-piece to enable weak patients
to pull themselves into a sitting posture. To the left of these
beds is a large glass double door which opens on to the
ground: one of the doors is open and a lovely September
sun, which is setting, gives a glow to the garden.

Through the door two poplar trees can be seen
silhouetted against the sky. To the right of this door is
another bed covered with a black quilt. Little white discs
are fixed to the head of each bed: on the first is the
number 26, on the second 27, and on the third 28.
Medical charts hang over each on the wall. To the right
is the fireplace, facing down the ward. Farther on, to the
right of the fire, is a door of a bathroom. In the corner,
between the glass door and the fire, is a pedestal on
which stands a statue of the Blessed Virgin; under the
statue is written, 'Mater Misericordiae, ora pro nobis'.
An easy chair, on which are rugs, is near the fire. In the
centre is a white, glass-topped table on which are
medicines, drugs, and surgical instruments. On one
corner is a vase of flowers. A locker is beside the head,
and a small chair by the foot of each bed. Two electric
lights, green shaded, hang from the ceiling, and a bracket
light with a red shade projects from the wall over the
fireplace. It is dusk, and the two lights suspended from
the ceiling are lighted. The walls are a brilliant white.

Sylvester is in the bed numbered 26; he is leaning upon his elbow looking towards the glass door.

Simon, sitting down on the chair beside bed numbered 27, is looking into the grounds.

Sylvester (*after a pause*) Be God, isn't it a good one!

Simon Almost, almost, mind you, Sylvester, incomprehensible.

Sylvester To come here and find Susie Monican fashion'd like a Queen of Sheba. God moves in a mysterious way, Simon.

Simon There's Surgeon Maxwell prancing after her now.

Sylvester (*stretching to see*) Heads together, eh? Be God, he's kissing her behind the trees! Oh, Susannah, Susannah, how are the mighty fallen, and the weapons of war perished!

Harry Heegan enters, crouched in a self-propelled invalid chair; he wheels himself up to the fire. Sylvester slides down into the bed, and Simon becomes interested in a book that he takes off the top of his locker. Harry remains for a few moments beside the fire, and then wheels himself round and goes out as he came in; Sylvester raises himself in the bed, and Simon leaves down the book to watch Harry.

Down and up, up and down.

Simon Up and down, down and up.

Sylvester Never quiet for a minute.

Simon Never able to hang on to an easy second.

Sylvester Trying to hold on to the little finger of life.

Simon Halfway up to heaven.

Sylvester And him always thinking of Jessie.

54

Simon And Jessie never thinking of him.

Susie Monican, in the uniform of a VAD nurse, enters the ward by the glass door. She is changed, for it is clear that she has made every detail of the costume as attractive as possible. She has the same assertive manner, but dignity and a sense of importance have been added. Her legs encased in silk stockings, are seen (and shown) to advantage by her short and smartly cut skirt. Altogether she is now a very handsome woman. Coming in she glances at the bed numbered 28, then pauses beside Sylvester and Simon.

Susie How is Twenty-Eight?

Simon *and* **Sylvester** (*together*) Travelling again.

Susie Did he speak at all to you?

Sylvester Dumb, Susie, dumb.

Simon Brooding, Susie; brooding, brooding.

Sylvester Cogitatin', Susie; cogitatin', cogitatin'.

Susie (*sharply, to Sylvester*) It's rediculous, Twenty-Six, for you to be in bed. The Sister's altogether too indulgent to you. Why didn't you pair of lazy devils entice him down to sit and cogitate under the warm wing of the sun in the garden?

Sylvester Considerin' the low state of his general health –

Simon Aided by a touch of frost in the air –

Sylvester Thinkin' it over we thought it might lead –

Simon To him getting an attack of double pneumonia.

Simon *and* **Sylvester** (*together*) An' then he'd go off like – (*They blow through their lips.*) Poof – the snuff of a candle!

Susie For the future, during the period you are patients here, I am to be addressed as 'Nurse Monican', and not as 'Susie'. Remember that, the pair of you, please.

Harry wheels himself in again, crossing by her, and, going over to the fire, looks out into grounds.

(*Irritatedly, to Sylvester*) Number Twenty-Six, look at the state of your quilt. You must make an effort to keep it tidy. Dtch, dtch, dtch, what would the Matron say if she saw it!

Simon (*with a nervous giggle*) He's an uneasy divil, Nurse Monican.

Susie (*hotly, to Simon*) Yours is as bad as his, Twenty-Seven. You mustn't lounge on your bed; it must be kept perfectly tidy. (*She smoothes the quilts.*) Please don't make it necessary to mention this again. (*To Harry.*) Would you like to go down for a little while into the garden, Twenty-Eight?

Harry crouches silent and moody.

After the sober rain of yesterday, it is good to feel the new grace of the yellowing trees, and to get the fresh smell of the grass.

Harry wheels himself round and goes out by the left.

(*To Sylvester as she goes out.*) Remember, Twenty-Six, if you're going to remain in a comatose condition, you'll have to keep your bed presentable.

A pause.

Sylvester (*mimicking Susie*) Twenty-Six, if you're going to remeen in a comatowse condition, you'll have to keep your bed in a tidy an' awdahly mannah.

Simon Dtch, dtch, dtch, Twenty-Seven, it's disgriceful. And as long as you're heah, in the capacity of a patient, please remember I'm not to be addressed as 'Susie', but as 'Nurse Monican'.

Sylvester Twenty-Seven, did you tike the pills the doctah awdahed?

Voice of Susie (*left*) Twenty-Six!

Sylvester Yes, Nurse?

Voice of Susie Sister says you're to have a bawth at once; and you, Twenty-Seven, see about getting it ready for him.

A fairly long pause.

Sylvester (*angrily*) A bawth: well, be God, that's a good one! I'm not in a fit condition for a bath!

Another pause.

(*Earnestly, to Simon.*) You haven't had a dip now for nearly a week, while I had one only the day before yesterday in the late evening: it must have been you she meant, Simon.

Simon Oh, there was no dubiety about her bellowing out Twenty-Six, Syl.

Sylvester (*excitedly*) How the hell d'ye know, man, she didn't mix the numbers up?

Simon Mix the numbers up! How could the woman mix the numbers up?

Sylvester How could the woman mix the numbers up! What could be easier than to say Twenty-Six instead of Twenty-Seven? How could the woman mix the numbers up! Of course the woman could mix the numbers up!

Simon What d'ye expect me to do – hurl myself into a bath that was meant for you?

Sylvester I don't want you to hurl yourself into anything;

but you don't expect me to plunge into a bath that maybe wasn't meant for me?

Simon Nurse Monican said Twenty-Six, and when you can alter that, ring me up and let me know.

A pause; then Simon gets up and goes towards bathroom door.

Sylvester (*snappily*) Where are you leppin' to now?

Simon I want to get the bath ready.

Sylvester You want to get the bawth ready! Turn the hot cock on, and turn the cold cock on for Number Twenty-Six, mixin' them the way a chemist would mix his medicines – sit still, man, till we hear the final verdict.

    Simon sits down again. Susie comes in left, and, passing to the door leading to grounds, pauses beside Simon and Sylvester.

Susie (*sharply*) What are the two of you doing? Didn't I tell you, Twenty-Six, that you were to take a bawth; and you, Twenty-Seven, that you were to get it ready for him?

Sylvester (*sitting brightly up in bed*) Oh, just goin' to spring up, Nurse Monican, when you popped in.

Susie Well, up with you, then, and take it. (*To Simon.*) You go and get it ready for him.

    Simon goes into the bathroom.

Sylvester (*venturing a last hope as Susie goes towards the entrance to grounds*) I had a dip, Nurse, only the day before yesterday in the late evening.

Susie (*as she goes out*) Have another one now, please.

    The water can be heard flowing in the bathroom, and a light cloud of steam comes out by the door, which Simon has left open.

Sylvester (*mimicking Susie*) 'Have another one, now, please! One to be taken before and after meals.' The delicate audacity of the lip of that one since she draped her shoulders with a crimson cape!

Simon appears and stands leaning against the side of the bathroom door.

Simon (*gloating*) She's steaming away now, Sylvester, full cock.

Sylvester (*scornfully, to Simon*) Music to you, the gurgling of the thing, music to you. Gaugin' the temperature for me. Dtch, dtch, dtch. (*Sitting up.*) An hospital's the last place that God made. Be damn it, I wouldn't let a stuffed bird stay in one!

Simon Come on, man, before the hot strength bubbles out of it.

Sylvester (*getting out of bed*) Have you the towels hot an' everything ready for me to spring into?

Simon (*with a bow*) Everything's ready for your enjoyment, sir.

Sylvester (*as he goes towards the bathroom*) Can't they be content with an honest to God cleanliness, an' not be tryin' to gild a man with soap and water.

Simon (*with a grin, as Sylvester passes*) Can I do anything more for you, sir?

Sylvester (*almost inarticulate with indignation, as he goes in*) Now I'm tellin' you, Simon Norton, our cordiality's gettin' a little strained!

Harry wheels himself in, goes again to the fireplace, and looks into grounds. Simon watches him for a moment, takes a package of cigarettes from his pocket and lights one.

Simon (*awkwardly, to Harry*) Have a fag, Harry, oul' son?

Harry Don't want one; tons of my own in the locker.

Simon Like me to get you one?

Harry I can get them myself if I want one. D'ye think my arms are lifeless as well as my legs?

Simon Far from that. Everybody's remarking what a great improvement has taken place in you during the last few days.

Harry Everybody but myself.

Simon What with the rubbing every morning and the rubbing every night, and now the operation tomorrow as a grand fin-ally, you'll maybe be in the centre of the football field before many months are out.

Harry (*irritably*) Oh, shut up, man! It's a miracle I want – not an operation. The last operation was to give life to my limbs, but no life came, and again I felt the horrible sickness of life only from the waist up. (*Raising his voice.*) Don't stand there gaping at me, man. Did you never before clap your eyes on a body dead from the belly down? Blast you, man, why don't you shout at me, 'While there's life there's hope!'

Simon edges away to his corner. Susie comes in by the glass door and goes over to the table.

(*To Susie.*) A package of fags. Out of the locker. Will you, Susie?

Susie goes to Harry's locker, gets the cigarettes and gives them to him. As he lights the cigarette, his right arm gives a sudden jerk.

Susie Steady. What's this?

Harry (*with a nervous laugh*) Barred from my legs it's flowing back into my arms. I can feel it slyly creeping into my fingers.

Voice of Patient (*out left, plaintively*) Nurse!

Susie (*turning her head in direction of the voice*) Shush, you, Twenty-Three; go asleep, go asleep.

Harry A soft, velvety sense of distance between my fingers and the things I touch.

Susie Stop thinking of it. Brooding checks the chance of your recovery. A good deal may be imagination.

Harry (*peevishly*) Oh, I know the different touches of iron – (*He touches the bed rail.*) Of wood – (*He touches the chair.*) Of flesh – (*He touches his cheek*). And to my fingers they're giving the same answers – a feeling of numb distance between me and the touches of them all.

Voice of Patient (*out left, plaintively*) Nurse!

Susie Dtch, dtch. Go asleep, Twenty-Three.

Voice of Patient (*out left*) The stab in the head is worse than ever, Nurse.

Susie You've got your dose of morphia, and you'll get no more. You'll just have to stick it.

Resident Surgeon Forby Maxwell enters from the grounds. He is about thirty years of age, and good-looking. His white overalls are unbuttoned, showing war ribbons on his waistcoat, flanked by the ribbon of the DSO. He has a careless, jaunty air, and evidently takes a decided interest in Susie. He comes in singing softly.

Surgeon Maxwell (*singing*)
Stretched on the couch, Jessie fondled her dress,
That hid all her beauties just over the knee;
And I wondered and said, as I sigh'd, 'What a shame,
That there's no room at all on the couch there for me.'

Susie (*to Surgeon Maxwell*) Twenty-Three's at it again.

Surgeon Maxwell Uh, hopeless case. Half his head in Flanders. May go on like that for another month.

Susie He keeps the patients awake at night.

Simon With his 'God have mercys on me', running after every third or fourth tick of the clock.

Harry 'Tisn't fair to me, 'tisn't fair to me; I must get my bellyful of sleep if I'm ever going to get well.

Surgeon Maxwell Oh, the poor devil won't trouble any of you much longer.

Singing:

Said Jess, with a light in the side of her eyes,
'A shrewd, mathematical fellow like you,
With an effort of thought should be able to make
The couch wide enough for the measure of two.'

Susie Dtch, dtch, Surgeon Maxwell.

Surgeon Maxwell (*singing*)
I fixed on a plan, and I carried it through,
And the eyes of Jess gleam'd as she whisper'd to me:
'The couch, made for one, that was made to hold two,
Has, maybe, been made big enough to hold three!'

Surgeon Maxwell catches Susie's hand in his. Sylvester bursts in from the bathroom, and rushes to his bed, colliding with the Surgeon as he passes him.

Hallo, hallo there, what's this?

Sylvester (*flinging himself into bed, covering himself rapidly with the clothes, blowing himself warm*) Pooh, pooh, I feel as if I was sittin' on the doorstep of pneumonia! Pooh, oh!

Surgeon Maxwell (*to Sylvester*) We'll have a look at you in a moment, Twenty-Six, and see what's wrong with you.

Sylvester subsides down into the bed. Simon edges towards the entrance to grounds, and stands looking into the grounds, or watching Surgeon Maxwell examining Sylvester.

(*To Harry, who is looking intently out into the grounds.*) Well, how are we today, Heegan?

Harry I imagine I don't feel quite so dead in myself as I've felt these last few days back.

Surgeon Maxwell Oh, well, that's something.

Harry Sometimes I think I feel a faint, fluttering kind of a buzz in the tops of my thighs.

Surgeon Maxwell (*touching Harry's thigh*) Where, here?

Harry No; higher up, doctor; just where the line is that leaves the one part living and the other part dead.

Surgeon Maxwell A buzz?

Harry A timid, faint, fluttering kind of a buzz.

Surgeon Maxwell That's good. There might be a lot in that faint, fluttering kind of a buzz.

Harry (*after a pause*) I'm looking forward to the operation tomorrow.

Surgeon Maxwell That's the way to take it. While there's life there's hope. (*With a grin and a wink at Susie.*) And now we'll have a look at Twenty-Six.

Harry, when he hears 'While there's life there's hope', wheels himself madly out left; halfway out he turns his head and stretches to look out into the grounds, then he goes on.

Susie Will the operation tomorrow be successful?

Surgeon Maxwell Oh, of course; very successful.

Susie Do him any good, d'ye think?

Surgeon Maxwell Oh, blast the good it'll do him.

Susie goes over to Sylvester in the bed.

Susie (*to Sylvester*) Sit up, Twenty-Six, Surgeon Maxwell wants to examine you.

Sylvester (*sitting up with a brave effort but a woeful smile*) Righto. In the pink!

Surgeon Maxwell comes over, twirling his stethoscope. Simon peeps round the corner of the glass door.

Susie (*to Surgeon Maxwell*) What was the cause of the row between the Matron and Nurse Jennings? (*To Sylvester.*) Open your shirt, Twenty-Six.

Surgeon Maxwell (*who has fixed the stethoscope in his ears, removing it to speak to Susie*) Caught doing the tango in the Resident's arms in the Resident's room. Naughty girl, naughty girl. (*To Sylvester*) Say 'ninety-nine'.

Sylvester Ninety-nine.

Susie Oh, I knew something like that would happen. Daughter of a Dean, too.

Surgeon Maxwell (*to Sylvester*) Say 'ninety-nine'.

Sylvester Ninety-nine. U-u-uh, it's gettin' very cold here, sitting up!

Surgeon Maxwell (*to Sylvester*) Again. Don't be frightened; breathe quietly.

Sylvester Ninety-nine. Cool as a cucumber, Doctor. Ninety-nine.

Surgeon Maxwell (*to Susie*) Damn pretty little piece. Not so pretty as you, though.

Sylvester (*to Surgeon Maxwell*) Yesterday Dr Joyce, givin' me a run over, said to a couple of medical men that were with him lookin' for tips, that the thing was apparently yieldin' to treatment, and that an operation wouldn't be necessary.

Surgeon Maxwell Go on; ninety-nine, ninety-nine.

Sylvester Ninety-nine, ninety-nine.

Surgeon Maxwell (*to Susie*) Kicks higher than her head, and you should see her doing the splits.

Sylvester (*to Surgeon Maxwell*) Any way of gettin' rid of it'll do for me, for I'm not one of them that'll spend a night before an operation in a crowd of prayers.

Susie Not very useful things to be doing and poor patients awaiting attention.

Surgeon Maxwell (*putting stethoscope into pocket*) He'll do alright; quite fit. Great old skin. (*To Sylvester.*) You can cover yourself up, now. (*To Susie.*) And don't tell me, Nurse Susie, that you've never felt a thrill or left a bedside for a kiss in a corner. (*He tickles her under the arm.*) Kiss in a corner, Nurse!

Susie (*pleased, but coy*) Please don't, Dr Maxwell, please.

Surgeon Maxwell (*tickling her again as they go out*) Kiss in a corner; ta-ra-ra-ra, kiss in a corner!

A pause.

Sylvester (*to Simon*) Simon, were you listenin' to that conversation?

Simon Indeed I was.

Sylvester We have our hands full, Simon, to keep alive. Think of sinkin' your body to the level of a hand that, ta-ra-ra-ra, would plunge a knife into your middle, haphazard, hurryin' up to run away after a thrill from a kiss in a corner. Did you see me dizzied an' wastin' me time pumpin' ninety-nines out of me, unrecognised, quiverin' with cold an' equivocation!

Simon Everybody says he's a very clever fellow with the knife.

Sylvester He'd gouge out your eye, saw off your arm, lift a load of vitals out of your middle, rub his hands, keep down a terrible desire to cheer lookin' at the ruin, an' say, 'Twenty-Six, when you're a little better, you'll feel a new man!'

> *Mrs Heegan, Mrs Foran and Teddy enter from the grounds. Mrs Foran is leading Teddy, who has a heavy bandage over his eyes, and is dressed in the blue clothes of military hospitals.*

Mrs Foran (*to Teddy*) Just a little step here, Ted; upsh! That's it; now we're on the earth again, beside Simon and Sylvester. You'd better sit here.

> *She puts him sitting on a chair.*

Sylvester (*to Mrs Heegan, as she kisses him*) Well, how's the old woman, eh?

Mrs Heegan A little anxious about poor Harry.

Simon He'll be alright. Tomorrow'll tell a tale.

Susie (*coming in, annoyed*) Who let you up here at this hour? Twenty-Eight's to have an operation tomorrow, and shouldn't be disturbed.

Mrs Heegan Sister Peter Alcantara said we might come up, Nurse.

Mrs Foran (*loftily*) Sister Peter Alcantara's authority ought to be good enough, I think.

Mrs Heegan Sister Peter Alcantara said a visit might buck him up a bit.

Mrs Foran Sister Peter Alcantara knows the responsibility she'd incur by keeping a wife from her husband and a mother from her son.

Susie Sister Peter Alcantara hasn't got to nurse him. And remember, nothing is to be said that would make his habit of introspection worse than it is.

Mrs Foran (*with dignity*) Thanks for the warnin', Nurse, but them kind of mistakes is unusual with us.

Susie goes out left, as Harry wheels himself rapidly in. Seeing the group, he stops suddenly, and a look of disappointment comes on to his face.

Mrs Heegan (*kissing Harry*) How are you, son?

Mrs Foran I brought Teddy, your brother in arms, up to see you, Harry.

Harry (*impatiently*) Where's Jessie? I thought you were to bring her with you?

Mrs Heegan She's comin' after us in a moment.

Harry Why isn't she here now?

Mrs Foran She stopped to have a word in the grounds with someone she knew.

Harry It was Barney Bagnal, was it? Was it Barney Bagnal?

Teddy Maybe she wanted to talk to him about gettin' the VC.

Harry What VC? Who's gettin' the VC?

Teddy Barney. Did he not tell you?

Mrs Foran prods his knee.

What's up?

Harry (*intensely, to Teddy*) What's he gettin' it for? What's he gettin' the VC for?

Teddy For carryin' you wounded out of the line of fire.

Mrs Foran prods his knee.

What's up?

Harry (*in anguish*) Christ Almighty, for carryin' me wounded out of the line of fire!

Mrs Heegan (*rapidly*) Harry, I wouldn't be thinkin' of anything till we see what the operation 'll do tomorrow.

Simon (*rapidly*) God, if it gave him back the use even of one of his legs.

Mrs Foran (*rapidly*) Look at all the places he could toddle to, an' all the things he could do then with the prop of a crutch.

Mrs Heegan Even at the worst, he'll never be dependin' on anyone, for he's bound to get the maximum allowance.

Simon Two quid a week, isn't it?

Sylvester Yes, a hundred per cent total incapacitation.

Harry She won't come up if one of you don't go down and bring her up.

Mrs Heegan She's bound to come up, for she's got your ukelele.

Harry Call her up, Simon, call her up – I must see Jessie.

Simon goes over to the door leading to the grounds, and looks out.

Mrs Foran (*bending over till her face is close to Harry's*) The drawn look on his face isn't half as bad as when I seen him last.

Mrs Heegan (*bending and looking into Harry's face*) Look, the hollows under his eyes is fillin' up, too.

Teddy I'm afraid he'll have to put Jessie out of his head, for when a man's hit in the spine . . .

Mrs Foran prods his knee.

What's up, woman?

Harry (*impatiently, to Simon*) Is she coming? Can you see her anywhere?

Simon I see someone like her in the distance, under the trees.

Harry Call her; can't you give her a shout, man?

Simon (*calling*) Jessie. Is that you, Jessie! Jessie-e!

Mrs Heegan (*to Harry*) What time are you goin' under the operation?

Harry (*to Simon*) Call her again, call her again, can't you!

Simon (*calling*) Jessie; Jessie-e!

Teddy Not much of a chance for an injury to the spine, for . . .

Mrs Foran (*putting her face close to Teddy's*) Oh, shut up, you!

Harry Why did you leave her in the grounds? Why didn't you wait till she came up with you?

Mrs Foran (*going over to Simon and calling*) Jessie, Jessie-e!

Jessie's Voice (*in distance*) Yehess!

Mrs Foran (*calling*) Come up here at once; we're all waitin' for you!

Jessie's Voice I'm not going up!

Mrs Foran (*calling*) Bring up that ukelele here at once, miss!

Jessie's Voice Barney'll bring it up!

Harry, who has been listening intently, wheels himself rapidly to where Simon and Mrs Foran are, pushing through them hurriedly.

Harry (*calling loudly*) Jessie! Jessie! Jessie-e!

Mrs Foran Look at that, now; she's runnin' away, the young rip!

Harry (*appealingly*) Jessie! Jessie-e!

Susie enters quickly from left. She goes over to Harry and pulls him back from the door.

Susie (*indignantly*) Disgraceful! Rousing the whole ward with this commotion! Dear, dear, dear, look at the state of Twenty-Eight. Come along, come along, please; you must all go at once.

Harry Jessie's coming up for a minute, Nurse.

Susie No more to come up. We've had enough for one night, and you for a serious operation tomorrow. Come on, all out, please.

She conducts Mrs Heegan, Mrs Foran, and Teddy out left.

Mrs Foran (*going out*) We're goin', we're goin', thank you. A nice way to treat the flotsum and jetsum of the battlefields!

Susie (*to Harry*) To bed now, Twenty-Eight, please. (*To Simon.*) Help me get him to bed, Twenty-Seven.

Susie pushes Harry to his bed, right; Simon brings a portion of a bed-screen which he places around Harry,

hiding him from view. She turns to speak to Sylvester,
who is sitting up in bed, as she arranges screen.

You're going to have your little operation in the morning,
so you'd better go to sleep too.

Sylvester goes pale and a look of dismay and fear
crawls over his face.

Don't funk it now. They're not going to turn you inside
out. It'll be over in ten minutes.

Sylvester (*with a groan*) When they once get you down
your only hope is in the infinite mercy of God!

Simon If I was you, Sylvester, I wouldn't take this
operation too seriously. You know th' oul' song – 'Let
Me Like a Soldier Fall'! If I was you, I'd put it completely
out of me mind.

Sylvester (*subsiding on to the pillow – with an agonised*
look on his face) Let me like a soldier fall! Did anyone
ever hear th' equal o' that! Put it out of me mind
completely!

He sits up, and glares at Simon.

Eh, you, look! If you can't think sensibly, then thry to
think without talkin'!

He sinks back on the pillow again.

'Let me like a soldier fall'. Oh, it's not a fair trial for a
sensible man to be stuck down in a world like this!

Sylvester slides down till he lies prone and motionless
on the bed. Harry is in bed now. Simon removes the
screen, and Susie arranges Harry's quilt for the night.

Susie (*to Simon*) Now run and help get the things together
for supper.

Simon goes out left.

(*Encouragingly to Harry.*) After the operation, a stay in the air of the Convalescent may work wonders.

Harry If I could mingle my breath with the breeze that blows from every sea, and over every land, they wouldn't widen me into anything more than the shrivell'd thing I am.

Susie switches off the two hanging lights, so that the red light over the fireplace alone remains.

Susie Don't be foolish, Twenty-Eight. Wheeling yourself about among the beeches and the pines, when the daffodils are hanging out their blossoms, you'll deepen your chance in the courage and renewal of the country.

The bell of a Convent in the grounds begins to ring for Compline.

Harry (*with intense bitterness*) I'll say to the pine, 'Give me the grace and beauty of the beech'; I'll say to the beech, 'Give me the strength and stature of the pine'. In a net I'll catch butterflies in bunches; twist and mangle them between my fingers and fix them wriggling on to mercy's banner. I'll make my chair a juggernaut, and wheel it over the neck and spine of every daffodil that looks at me, and strew them dead to manifest the mercy of God and the justice of man!

Susie (*shocked*) Shush, Harry, Harry!

Harry To hell with you, your country, trees, and things, you jibbering jay!

Susie (*as she is going out*) Twenty-Eight!

Harry (*vehemently*) To hell with you, your country, trees, and things, you jibbering jay!

Susie looks at him, pauses for a few moments, as if to speak, and then goes out.

A pause; then Barney comes in by the door from the grounds. An overcoat covers his military hospital uniform of blue. His left arm is in a sling. Under his right arm he carries a ukelele, and in his hand he has a bunch of flowers. Embarrassed, he goes slowly to Harry's bed, drops the flowers at the foot, then he drops the ukelele there.

Barney (*awkwardly*) Your ukelele. An' a bunch of flowers from Jessie.

Harry remains motionless on the bed.

A bunch of flowers from Jessie, and . . . your . . . ukelele.

The Sister of the Ward enters, left, going to the chapel for Compline. She wears a cream habit with a white coif; a large set of rosary beads hangs from her girdle. She pauses on her way, and a brass crucifix flashes on her bosom.

Sister (*to Harry*) Keeping brave and hopeful, Twenty-Eight?

Harry (*softly*) Yes, Sister.

Sister Splendid. And we've got a ukelele too. Can you play it, my child?

Harry Yes, Sister.

Sister Splendid. You must play me something when you're well over the operation. (*To Barney.*) Standing guard over your comrade, Twenty-Two, eh?

Barney (*softly and shyly*) Yes, Sister.

Sister Grand. Forasmuch as ye do it unto the least of these my brethren, ye do it unto me. Well, God be with you both, my children. (*To Harry.*) And Twenty-Eight, pray to God, for wonderful He is in His doing toward the children of men.

She is calm and dignified she goes out into the grounds.

Barney (*pausing as he goes out left*) They're on the bed; the ukelele, and the bunch of flowers from . . . Jessie.

The Sisters are heard singing in the convent the hymn of Salve Regina.

Sisters (*singing*)
Salve Regina, mater misericordiae;
Vitae dulcedo et spes nostra, salve!
Ad te clamamus, exules filii Hevae;
Ad te suspiramus, gementes et flentes in hac lacrymarum
    valle.
Eia ergo Advocata nostra,
Illos tuos misericordes oculos ad nos converte,
Et Jesum, benedictum fructum ventris tui –

Harry God of the miracles, give a poor devil a chance, give a poor devil a chance!

Sisters (*singing*)
Nobis post hoc exsilium ostende,
O clemens, o pia, o dulcis Virgo Maria!

End of Act Three.

Act Four

A room of the dance hall of the Avondale Football Club.
At back, left, cutting corners of the back and side walls, is
the arched entrance, divided by a slim pillar, to the dance
hall. This entrance is hung with crimson and black striped
curtains; whenever these are parted the dancers can be
seen swinging or gliding past the entrance if a dance be
taking place at the time. Over the entrance is a scroll on
which is printed: 'Up the Avondales!' The wall back has a
wide, tall window which opens to the garden, in which the
shrubs and some sycamore trees can be seen. It is hung
with apple-green casement curtains, which are pulled to
the side to allow the window to be open as it is at present.
Between the entrance to hall and the window is a Roll of
Honour containing the names of five members of the Club
killed in the war. Underneath the Roll of Honour a wreath
of laurel tied with red and black ribbon. To the front left is
the fireplace. Between the fireplace and the hall entrance
is a door on which is an oval white enamel disc with
CARETAKER *painted on it. To the right a long table, covered*
with a green cloth, on which are numerous bottles of wine
and a dozen glasses. On the table, too, is a telephone.
A brown carpet covers the floor. Two easy chairs and one
ordinary are in the room. Hanging from the ceiling are
three lanterns; the centre one is four times the length of
its width, the ones at the side are less than half as long as
the centre lantern and hang horizontally; the lanterns are
black, with a broad red stripe running down the centre of
the largest and across those hanging at each side, so that,
when they are lighted, they suggest an illuminated black
cross with an inner one of gleaming red.

*The hall is vividly decorated with many coloured
lanterns, looped with coloured streamers. When the scene
is revealed the curtains are drawn, and the band can be
heard playing a foxtrot. Outside in the garden, near the
window, Simon and Sylvester can be seen smoking, and
Teddy is walking slowly up and down the path. The band
is heard playing for a few moments, then the curtains are
pulled aside, and Jessie, with Barney holding her hand,
comes in and walks rapidly to the table where the wine is
standing. They are quickly followed by Harry, who wheels
himself a little forward, then stops, watching them. The
curtains part again, and Mrs Heegan is seen watching
Harry. Simon and Sylvester, outside, watch those in the
room through the window. Barney wears a neat navy-blue
suit, with a rather high, stiff collar and black tie. Pinned
on the breast of his waistcoat are his war medals, flanked
by the Victoria Cross. Harry is also wearing his medals.
Jessie has on a very pretty, rather tight-fitting dance
frock, with the sleeves falling widely to the elbow, and
cut fairly low on her breast. All the dancers, and Harry
too, wear coloured, fantastically shaped paper hats.*

*Jessie is hot, excited, and uneasy, as with a rapid glance
back she sees the curtains parted by Harry.*

Jessie Here he comes prowling after us again! His
watching of us is pulling all the enjoyment out of the
night. It makes me shiver to feel him wheeling after us.

Barney We'll watch for a chance to shake him off, an' if
he starts again we'll make him take his tangled body
somewhere else.

As Harry moves forward from the curtained entrance.

Shush, he's comin' near us. (*In a louder tone to Jessie.*)
Red wine, Jessie, for you, or white wine?

Harry Red wine first, Jessie, to the passion and the power
and the pain of life, an' then a drink of white wine to the
melody that is in them all!

76

Jessie I'm so hot.

Harry I'm so cold; white wine for the woman warm to make her cold; red wine for the man that's cold to make him warm!

Jessie White wine for me.

Harry For me the red wine till I drink to men puffed up with pride of strength, for even creeping things can praise the Lord!

Barney (*gently to Harry, as he gives a glass of wine to Jessie*) No more for you now, Harry.

Harry (*mockingly*) Oh, please, your lusty lordship, just another, an' if I seek a second, smack me well.

He wheels his chair viciously against Barney.

Get out, you trimm'd-up clod. There's medals on my breast as well as yours! (*He fills a glass.*)

Jessie Let us go back to the dancing, Barney.

Barney hesitates.

Please, Barney, let us go back to the dancing!

Harry To the dancing, for the day cometh when no man can play. And legs were made to dance, to run, to jump, to carry you from one place to another; but mine can neither walk, nor run, nor jump, nor feel the merry motion of a dance. But stretch me on the floor fair on my belly, and I will turn over on my back, then wriggle back again on to my belly; and that's more than a dead, dead man can do!

Barney Jessie wants to dance, an' so we'll go, and leave you here a little.

Harry Cram pain with pain, and pleasure cram with pleasure. I'm going too. You'd cage me in from seeing you dance, and dance, and dance, with Jessie close to you, and you so close to Jessie. Though you wouldn't think it, yes, I have – I've hammer'd out many a merry measure upon a polish'd floor with a sweet, sweet heifer.

As Barney and Jessie are moving away he catches hold of Jessie's dress.

Her name? Oh, any name will do – we'll call her Jessie!

Jessie Oh, let me go. (*To Barney.*) Barney, make him let me go, please.

Barney, without a word, removes Harry's hand from Jessie's dress. Jessie and Barney then go out to the dance hall through the curtained entrance. After a while Mrs Heegan slips away from the entrance into the hall. After a moment's pause Harry follows them into the hall. Simon and Sylvester come in from the garden, leaving Teddy still outside smoking and walking to and fro in the cautious manner of the blind. Simon and Sylvester sit down near the fire and puff in silence for a few moments.

Sylvester (*earnestly*) I knew it. I knew it, Simon – strainin', an' strainin' his nerves; driftin', an' driftin' towards an hallucination!

Simon Jessie might try to let him down a little more gently, but it would have been better, I think, if Harry hadn't come here tonight.

Sylvester I concur in that, Simon. What's a decoration to an hospital is an anxiety here.

Simon To carry life and colour to where there's nothing but the sick and helpless is right; but to carry the sick and helpless to where there's nothing but life and colour is wrong.

The telephone bell rings.

78

Sylvester There's the telephone bell ringing.

Simon Oh, someone'll come in and answer it in a second.

Sylvester To join a little strength to a lot of weakness is what I call sensible; but to join a little weakness to a lot of strength is what I call a . . .

Simon A cod.

Sylvester Exactly.

The telephone continues to ring.

There's that telephone ringin' still.

Simon Oh, someone 'll come in and answer it in a second.

Teddy has groped his way to the French window.

Teddy The telephone's tinklin', boys.

Sylvester Thanks, Teddy. We hear it, thanks. (*To Simon.*) When he got the invitation from the Committay to come, wearin' his decorations, me an' the old woman tried to persuade him that, seein' his condition, it was better to stop at home, an' let me represent him, but – (*with a gesture*) no use!

Teddy resumes his walk to and fro.

Simon It was natural he'd want to come, since he was the means of winning the Cup twice before for them, leading up to their keeping the trophy for ever by the win of a year ago.

Sylvester To bring a boy so helpless as him, whose memory of agility an' strength time hasn't flattened down, to a place wavin' with joy an' dancin', is simply, simply –

Simon Devastating, I'd say.

Sylvester Of course it is! Is that God-damn telephone goin' to keep ringin' all night?

Mrs Foran enters from hall quickly.

Mrs Foran Miss Monican says that one of you is to answer the telephone, an' call her if it's anything important.

Sylvester (*nervously*) I never handled a telephone in my life.

Simon I chanced it once and got so hot and quivery that I couldn't hear a word, and didn't know what I was saying myself.

Mrs Foran Have a shot at it and see.

The three of them drift over to the telephone.

Sylvester Chance it again, Simon, an' try to keep steady.

As Simon stretches his hand to the receiver.

Don't rush, don't rush, man, an' make a mess of it. Take it in your stride.

Simon (*pointing to receiver*) When you lift this down, you're connected, I think.

Sylvester No use of thinkin' on this job. Don't you turn the handle first?

Simon (*irritably*) No, you don't turn no handle, man!

Mrs Foran Let Simon do it now; Simon knows.

Simon tremblingly lifts down the receiver, almost letting it fall.

Sylvester Woah, woah, Simon; careful, careful!

Simon (*speaking in receiver*) Eh, hallo! Eh, listen there. Eh, hallo! Listen.

Sylvester You listen, man, an' give the fellow at the other end a chance to speak.

80

Simon If you want me to manipulate the thing, let me manipulate it in tranquillity.

Mrs Foran (*to Sylvester*) Oh, don't be puttin' him out, Sylvester.

Simon (*waving them back*) Don't be crushing in on me; give me room to manipulate the thing.

Dead silence for some moments.

Mrs Foran Are you hearin' anything from the other end?

Simon A kind of a buzzing and a roaring noise.

Sylvester suddenly gives the cord a jerk and pulls the receiver out of Simon's hand.

(*Angrily*) What the hell are you trying to do, man? You're after pulling it right out of my mit.

Sylvester (*heatedly*) There was a knot or a twist an' a tangle in it that was keepin' the sound from travellin'.

Simon If you want me to work the thing properly, you'll have to keep yourself from interfering. (*Resuming surlily.*) Eh, hallo, listen, yes? Ha! ha! ha! ha! Yes, yes, yes. No, no, no. Cheerio! Yes. Eh, hallo, listen, eh. Hallo.

Sylvester What is it? What're they sayin'?

Simon (*hopelessly, taking the receiver from his ear*) I don't seem to be able to hear a damn sound.

Sylvester An' Holy God, what are you yessin' and noin' and cheerioin' out of you for then?

Simon You couldn't stand here like a fool and say nothing, could you?

Sylvester Show it to me, Simon, show it to me – you're not holdin' it at the proper angle.

81

Mrs Foran Give it to Syl, Simon; it's a delicate contrivance that needs a knack in handlin'.

Sylvester (*as he is taking the receiver from Simon and carefully placing it to his ear*) You have always to preserve an eqwee-balance between the speakin' mouth and the hearin' ear. (*Speaking into receiver.*) Hallo! Anybody there at the other end of this? Eh, wha's that? Yes, yes, I've got you. (*Taking the receiver from his ear and speaking to Simon and Mrs Foran.*) Something like wine, or dine, or shine, or something – an' a thing that's hummin'.

Simon I can see no magnificent meaning jumping out of that!

Mrs Foran They couldn't be talkin' about bees, could they?

Sylvester (*scornfully*) Bees! No, they couldn't be talkin' about bees! That kind of talk, Mrs Foran, only tends to confuse matters. Bees! Dtch, dtch, dtch – the stupidity of some persons is . . . terrifyin'!

Simon Ask them quietly what they want.

Sylvester (*indignantly*) What the hell's the use of askin' them that, when I can hear something only like a thing that's hummin'?

Mrs Foran It wouldn't be, now, comin', or even bummin'?

Sylvester It might even possibly be drummin'. Personally, Mrs Foran, I think, since you can't help, you might try to keep from hinderin'.

Simon Put it back, Syl, where it was, an' if it rings again, we'll only have to slip quietly out of this.

Mrs Foran Yes, put it back, an' say it never rang.

Sylvester Where was it? Where do I put it back?

Simon On that thing stickin' out there. Nice and gently now.

Sylvester cautiously puts receiver back. They look at the telephone for a few moments, then go back to the fire, one by one. Sylvester stands with his back to it; Simon sits in a chair, over the back of which Mrs Foran leans.

Mrs Foran Curious those at the other end of the telephone couldn't make themselves understood.

Simon Likely they're not accustomed to it, and it's a bit difficult if you're not fully conscious of its manipulation.

Sylvester Well, let them study an' study it then, or abide by the consequences, for we can't be wastin' time teachin' them.

The curtains at entrance of dance hall are pulled aside, and Teddy, who has disappeared from the garden a little time before, comes in. As he leaves the curtains apart, the dancers can be seen gliding past the entrance in the movements of a tango. Teddy comes down, looks steadily but vacantly towards the group around the fire, then goes over carefully to the table, where he moves his hand about till it touches a bottle, which he takes up in one hand, feeling it questioningly from the other.

Simon How goes it, Teddy?

Teddy (*with a vacant look towards them*) Sylvester – Simon – well. What seest thou, Teddy? Thou seest not as man seeth. In the garden the trees stand up; the green things showeth themselves and fling out flowers of divers hues. In the sky the sun by day and the moon and the stars by night – nothing. In the hall the sound of dancing, the eyes of women, grey and blue and brown and black, do sparkle and dim and sparkle again. Their white breasts rise and fall, and rise again. Slender legs, from red and

83

black, and white and green, come out, go in again –
nothing. Strain as you may, it stretches from the throne
of God to the end of the hearth of hell.

Simon What?

Teddy The darkness.

Simon (*knowing not what to say*) Yes, oh yes.

Teddy (*holding up a bottle of wine*) What colour, Syl?
It's all the same, but I like the red the best.

Mrs Foran (*going over to Teddy*) Just one glass, dear,
and you'll sit down quietly an' take it in sips.

*Mrs Foran fills a glass of wine for Teddy, leads him
to a chair, puts him sitting down, and gives the glass of
wine carefully to him. The band in the hall has been
playing, and through the parted curtains the dancers
are seen gliding past. Jessie moves by now in the arms
of Barney, and in a few moments is followed along the
side of the hall by Harry wheeling himself in his chair
and watching them. Mrs Foran and the two men look
on and become more attentive when among the
dancers. Susie, in the arms of Surgeon Maxwell, Jessie
partnered with Barney, and Harry move past.*

Sylvester (*as Susie goes by*) Susie Monican's lookin' game
enough tonight for anything.

Simon Hardly remindful of her one-time fear of God.

Sylvester (*as Jessie goes by, followed by Harry*) There he
goes, still followin' them.

Simon And Jessie's looking as if she was tired of her
maidenhood, too.

Mrs Foran The thin threads holdin' her dress up sidelin'
down over her shoulders, an' her catchin' them up again
at the tail end of the second before it was too late.

Simon (*grinning*) And Barney's hand inching up, inching up to pull them a little lower when they're sliding down.

Mrs Foran Astonishin' the way girls are advertisin' their immodesty. Whenever one of them sits down, in my heart I pity the poor men havin' to view the disedifyin' sight of the full length of one leg couched over another.

Teddy (*forgetful*) A damn nice sight, all the same, I think.

Mrs Foran (*indignantly*) One would imagine such a thought would jar a man's mind that had kissed goodbye to the sight of his eyes.

Teddy Oh, don't be tickin' off every word I say!

After an astonished pause, Mrs Foran whips the glass out of Teddy's hand.

Mrs Foran Damn the drop more, now, you'll get for the rest of the evenin'.

The band suddenly stops playing, and the couples seen just then through the doorway stop dancing and look attentively up the hall. After a slight pause, Harry in his chair, pushed by Susie, comes in through the entrance; his face is pale and drawn, his breath comes in quick faint gasps, and his head is leaning sideways on the back of the chair. Mrs Heegan is on one side of Harry, and Surgeon Maxwell, who is in dinner-jacket style of evening dress, wearing his medals, including the DSO, walks on the other. Harry is wheeled over near the open window. Barney and Jessie, standing in the entrance, look on and listen.

Surgeon Maxwell Here near the window. (*To Mrs Heegan.*) He'll be all right, Mrs Heegan, in a second; a little faint – too much excitement. When he recovers a little, I'd get him home.

Harry (*faintly but doggedly*) Napoo home, napoo. Not

yet. I'm all right. I'll spend a little time longer in the belly of an hour bulgin' out with merriment. Carry on.

Surgeon Maxwell Better for you to go home, Heegan.

Harry When they drink to the Club from the Cup – the Silver Tassie – that I won three times, three times for them – that first was filled to wet the lips of Jessie and of me – I'll go, but not yet. I'm all right; my name is yet only a shadow on the Roll of Honour.

Mrs Heegan Come home, Harry; you're gettin' your allowance only on the understandin' that you take care of yourself.

Harry Get the Cup. I'll mind it here till you're ready to send it round to drink to the Avondales – on the table here beside me. Bring the Cup; I'll mind it here on the table beside me.

Surgeon Maxwell Get the Cup for him, someone.

Simon goes to the hall and returns with the Cup, which he gives to Harry.

Harry (*holding the Cup out*) A first drink again for me, for me alone this time, for the shell that hit me bursts for ever between Jessie and me. (*To Simon.*) Go on, man, fill out the wine!

Surgeon Maxwell (*to Simon*) A little – just a glass. Won't do him any harm. (*To Harry.*) Then you'll have to remain perfectly quiet, Heegan.

Harry The wine – fill out the wine!

Simon (*to Harry*) Red wine or white?

Harry Red wine, red like the faint remembrance of the fires in France; red wine like the poppies that spill their petals on the breasts of the dead men. No, white wine, white like the stillness of the millions that have removed their clamours from the crowd of life. No, red wine; red like the blood that was shed for you and for many for the commission of sin! (*He drinks the wine.*) Steady, Harry, and lift up thine eyes unto the hills. (*Roughly to those around him.*) What are you all gaping at?

Surgeon Maxwell Now, now, Heegan – you must try to keep quiet.

Susie And when you've rested and feel better, you will sing for us a Negro spiritual, and point the melody with the ukelele.

Mrs Heegan Just as he used to do.

Sylvester Behind the trenches.

Simon In the rest camps.

Mrs Foran Out in France.

Harry Push your sympathy away from me, for I'll have none of it.

He wheels his chair quickly towards the dance hall.

Go on with the dancing and keep the ball a-rolling. (*Calling loudly at the entrance.*) Trumpets and drum begin!

The band begins to play.

Dance and dance and dance. (*He listens for a moment.*) Sink into merriment again, and sling your cares to God!

He whirls round in the chair to the beat of the tune. Dancers are seen gliding past entrance.

Dear God, I can't. (*He sinks sideways on his chair.*) I must, must rest.

He quietly recites.

For a spell here I will stay,
Then pack up my body and go –

For mine is a life on the ebb,
Yours a full life on the flow!

*Harry goes over to far side of window and looks out
into garden. Mrs Heegan is on his right and Teddy on
his left; Simon and Sylvester a little behind, looking
on. Mrs Foran to the right of Mrs Heegan. Surgeon
Maxwell and Susie, who are a little to the front, watch
for a moment, then the Surgeon puts his arm round
Susie and the pair glide off into the dance hall.*

*When Surgeon Maxwell and Susie glide in to the
motions of the dance through the entrance into the
dance hall the curtains are pulled together. A few
moments' pause. Teddy silently puts his hand on
Harry's shoulder, and they both stare into the garden.*

Simon The air'll do him good.

Sylvester An' give him breath to sing his song an' play
the ukelele.

Mrs Heegan Just as he used to do.

Sylvester Behind the trenches.

Simon In the rest camps.

Mrs Foran Out in France.

Harry I can see, but I cannot dance.

Teddy I can dance, but I cannot see.

Harry Would that I had the strength to do the things
I see.

Teddy Would that I could see the things I've strength
to do.

Harry The Lord hath given and the Lord hath taken
away.

Teddy Blessed be the name of the Lord.

Mrs Foran I do love the ukelele, especially when it goes tinkle, tinkle, tinkle in the night-time.

Sylvester Bringin' before you glistenin' bodies of blacks, coilin' themselves an' shufflin' an' prancin' in a great jungle dance; shakin' assegais an' spears to the rattle, rattle, rattle an' thud, thud, thud of the tom-toms.

Mrs Foran There's only one possible musical trimmin' to the air of a Negro spiritual, an' that's the tinkle, tinkle, tinkle of a ukelele.

Harry The rising sap in trees I'll never feel.

Teddy The hues of branch or leaf I'll never see.

Harry There's something wrong with life when men can walk.

Teddy There's something wrong with life when men can see.

Harry I never felt the hand that made me helpless.

Teddy I never saw the hand that made me blind.

Harry Life came and took away the half of life.

Teddy Life took from me the half he left with you.

Harry The Lord hath given and the Lord hath taken away.

Teddy Blessed be the name of the Lord.

Susie comes quickly in by entrance, goes over to the table and, looking at several bottles of wine, selects one. She is going hurriedly back, when, seeing Harry, she goes over to him.

Susie (*kindly*) How are you now, Harry?

Harry All right, thank you.

Susie That's good.

Susie is about to hurry away, when Mrs Foran stops her with a remark.

Mrs Foran (*with a meaning gesture*) He's takin' it cushy till you're ready to hear him singin' his Negro spiritual, miss.

Susie Oh, God, I'd nearly forgotten that. They'll be giving out the balloons at the next dance, and when that foxtrot's over he'll have to come in and sing us the spiritual.

Mrs Heegan Just as he used to do.

Simon Behind the trenches.

Sylvester In the rest camps.

Mrs Foran Out of France.

Susie As soon as the balloon dance is over, Harry, out through the garden and in by the front entrance with you, so that you'll be ready to start as they all sit down. And after the song, we'll drink to the Club from the Silver Tassie.

She hurries back to the hall with the bottle of wine.

Mrs Foran I'm longin' to hear Harry on the ukelele.

Harry I hope I'll be able to do justice to it.

Mrs Heegan Of course you will, Harry.

Harry (*nervously*) Before a crowd. Forget a word and it's all up with you.

Simon Try it over now, softly; the sound couldn't carry as far as the hall.

Sylvester It'll give you confidence in yourself.

Harry (*to Simon*) Show us the ukelele, Simon.

Simon gets the ukelele and gives it to Harry.

Teddy If I knew the ukelele it might wean me a little way from the darkness.

Harry pulls a few notes, tuning the ukelele, then he softly sings.

Harry (*singing*)
Swing low, sweet chariot, comin' for to carry me home,
Swing low, sweet chariot, comin' for to carry me home,
I looked over Jordan, what did I see,
Comin' for to carry me home?
A band of angels comin' after me –
Comin' for to carry me home.

A voice in the hall is heard shouting through a megaphone:

Voice Balloons will be given out now! Given out now – the balloons!

Mrs Foran (*excitedly*) They're goin' to send up the balloons! They're going to let the balloons fly now!

Harry (*singing*)
Swing low, sweet chariot, comin' for to carry me home,
Swing low, sweet chariot, comin' for to carry me home.

Mrs Foran (*as Harry is singing*) Miss Monican wants us all to see the flyin' balloons.

She catches Teddy's arm and runs with him into the hall.

Simon We must all see the flyin' balloons.

Mrs Heegan (*running into hall*) Red balloons and black balloons.

Simon (*following Mrs Heegan*) Green balloons and blue balloons.

Sylvester (*following Simon*) Yellow balloons and puce balloons.

All troop into the hall, leaving the curtains apart, and Harry alone with his ukelele. Through the entrance various coloured balloons that have been tossed into the air can be seen, mid sounds of merriment and excitement.

Harry (*softly and slowly*) Comin' for to carry me home.

He throws the ukelele into an armchair, sits still for a moment, then goes to the table, takes up the silver cup, and wheels himself into the garden.
After a pause Barney looks in, then enters pulling Jessie by the hand, letting the curtains fall together again. Then he goes quickly to the window, shuts and bolts it, drawing to one half of the curtains, goes back to Jessie, catches her hand again, and tries to draw her towards room on the left. During the actions that follow the dance goes merrily on in the hall.

Jessie (*holding up a broken shoulder-strap and pulling back towards the hall*) Barney, no. God, I'd be afraid he might come in on us alone.

Hands part the curtains and throw in coloured streamers that encircle Jessie and Barney.

Barney Damn them! . . . He's gone, I tell you, to sing the song an' play the ukelele.

Jessie (*excited and afraid*) See, they're watching us. No, Barney. You mustn't. I'll not go!

Barney seizes Jessie in his arms and forces her towards the door on the left.

You wouldn't be good. I'll not go into that room.

Barney I will be good, I tell you! I just want to be alone with you for a minute.

He loosens Jessie's other shoulder-strap, so that her dress leaves her shoulders and bosom bare.

Jessie (*near the door left, as Barney opens it*) You've loosened my dress – I knew you weren't going to be good.

As she kisses him passionately:

Barney, Barney – you shouldn't be making me do what I don't want to do!

Barney (*holding her and trying to pull her into room*) Come on, Jessie, you needn't be afraid of Barney – we'll just rest a few minutes from the dancing.

At that part of the window uncurtained Harry is seen peering in. He then wheels his chair back and comes on to the centre of the window frame with a rush, bursting the catch and speeding into the room, coming to a halt, angry and savage, before Barney and Jessie.

Harry So you'd make merry over my helplessness in front of my face, in front of my face, you pair of cheats! You couldn't wait till I'd gone, so that my eyes wouldn't see the joy I wanted hurrying away from me over to another? Hurt her breast pulling your hand quick out of her bodice, did you? (*To Jessie.*) Saved you in the nick of time, my lady, did I? (*To Barney.*) Going to enjoy yourself on the same little couch where she, before you formed an image in her eye, acted the part of an amateur wife, and I acted the part of an amateur husband – the black couch with the green and crimson butterflies, in the yellow bushes, where she and me often tired of the things you're dangling after now!

Jessie He's a liar, he's a liar, Barney! He often tried it on with coaxing first and temper afterwards, but it always ended in a halt that left him where he started.

93

Harry If I had my hands on your white neck I'd leave marks there that crowds of kisses from your Barney wouldn't moisten away.

Barney You half-baked Lazarus, I've put up with you all the evening, so don't force me now to rough-handle the bit of life the Jerries left you as a souvenir!

Harry When I wanted to slip away from life, you brought me back with your whispered 'Think of the tears of Jess, think of the tears of Jess', but Jess has wiped away her tears in the ribbon of your Cross, and this poor crippled jest gives a flame of joy to the change; but when you get her, may you find in her the pressed down emptiness of a whore!

Barney (*running over and seizing Harry*) I'll tilt the leaking life out of you, you jealous, peering pimp!

Jessie (*trying to hold Barney back*) Barney, Barney, don't! don't!

Harry (*appealingly*) Barney, Barney! My heart – you're stopping it!

Jessie (*running to entrance and shouting in*) Help! help! They're killing each other!

In the hall the dance stops. Surgeon Maxwell runs in, followed by Susie, Simon, Sylvester, Mrs Foran, Mrs Heegan, and lastly Teddy, finding his way over to the window. Dancers gather around entrance and look on.

Surgeon Maxwell, running over, separates Barney from Harry.

Surgeon Maxwell What's this? Come, come – we can't have this sort of thing going on.

Mrs Heegan He was throttlin' him, throttlin' a poor helpless creature, an' if anything happens, he and that painted slug Jessie Taite 'll be held accountable!

94

Surgeon Maxwell This can't be allowed to go on. You'll have to bring him home. Any more excitement would be dangerous.

Mrs Heegan This is what he gets from Jessie Taite for sittin' on the stairs through the yawnin' hours of the night, racin' her off to the play an' the pictures, an' plungin' every penny he could keep from me into presents for the consolidation of the courtship!

Surgeon Maxwell Bring the boy home, woman, bring the boy home.

Sylvester (*fiercely to Jessie*) And money of mine in one of the gewgaws scintillatin' in her hair!

Jessie What gewgaw? What gewgaw?

Coloured streamers are thrown in by those standing at the entrance, which fall on and encircle some of the group around Harry.

Sylvester The tiarara I gave you two Christmases ago with the yellow berries and the three flutterin' crimson swallows.

Harry (*faintly and bitterly, with a hard little laugh*) Napoo Barney Bagnal and napoo Jessie Taite. A merry heart throbs coldly in my bosom; a merry heart in a cold bosom – or is it a cold heart in a merry bosom?

He gathers a number of the coloured streamers and winds them round himself and chair.

Teddy!

Harry catches Teddy by the sleeve and winds some more streamers round him.

Sing a song, man, and show the stuff you're made of!

Surgeon Maxwell (*catching hold of Mrs Heegan's arm*) Bring him home, woman.

He catches Sylvester's arm.

Get him home, man.

Harry Dear God, this crippled form is still your child.
(*To Mrs Heegan.*) Dear Mother, this helpless thing is still
your son. Harry Heegan, me, who, on the football field,
could crash a twelve-stone flyer off his feet. For this dear
Club three times I won the Cup, and grieve in reason I
was just too weak this year to play again. And now,
before I go, I give you all the Cup, the Silver Tassie, to
have and to hold for ever, evermore.

*From his chair he takes the Cup with the two sides
hammered close together, and holds it out to them.*

Mangled and bruised as I am bruised and mangled.
Hammered free from all its comely shape. Look, there is
Jessie writ, and here is Harry, the one name safely
separated from the other.

He flings it on the floor.

Treat it kindly. With care it may be opened out, for Barney
there to drink to Jess, and Jess there to drink to Barney.

Teddy Come, Harry, home to where the air is soft. No
longer can you stand upon a hill top; these empty eyes of
mine can never see from one. Our best is all behind us –
what's in front we'll face like men, dear comrade of the
blood fight and the battlefront!

Harry What's in front we'll face like men!

*Harry goes out by the window, Sylvester pushing the
chair, Teddy's hand on Harry's shoulder, Mrs Heegan
slowly following. Those left in the room watch them
going out through the garden, turning to the right till
they are all out of sight.*

(*As he goes out of window.*) The Lord hath given and
man hath taken away!

Teddy (*heard from the garden*) Blessed be the name of the Lord!

The band in the hall begins to play again. Those in the hall begin to dance.

Surgeon Maxwell Come on, all, we've wasted too much time already.

Susie (*to Jessie, who is sitting quietly in a chair*) Come on, Jessie – get your partner. (*Roguishly.*) You can have a quiet time with Barney later on.

Jessie Poor Harry!

Susie Oh nonsense! If you'd passed as many through your hands as I, you'd hardly notice one. (*To Jessie.*) Jessie, Teddy Foran and Harry Heegan have gone to live their own way in another world. Neither I nor you can lift them out of it. No longer can they do the things we do. We can't give sight to the blind or make the lame walk. We would if we could. It is the misfortune of war. As long as wars are waged, we shall be vexed by woe; strong legs shall be made useless and bright eyes made dark. But we, who have come through the fire unharmed, must go on living.

Pulling Jessie from the chair:

Come along, and take your part in life! (*To Barney.*) Come along, Barney, and take your partner into the dance!

Barney comes over, puts his arm round Jessie, and they dance into the hall. Susie and Surgeon Maxwell dance together. As they dance the waltz 'Over the Waves' some remain behind drinking. Two of these sing the song to the same tune as the dance.

Surgeon Maxwell
Swing into the dance,
Take joy when it comes, ere it go;

97

For the full flavour of life
Is either a kiss or a blow.
He to whom joy is a foe,
Let him wrap himself up in his woe;
For he is a life on the ebb,
We a full life on the flow!

All in the hall dance away with streamers and balloons flying. Simon and Mrs Foran sit down and watch the fun through the entrance. Mrs Foran lights a cigarette and smokes. A pause as they look on.

Mrs Foran It's a terrible pity Harry was too weak to stay an' sing his song, for there's nothing I love more than the ukelele's tinkle, tinkle in the night-time.

Curtain.

Song and Chants in
The Silver Tassie

1st CHANT

Intonation

I____ sees the mis-sus paryd-ing a-long Wal-ham Green, Through the jewels

Mediation

an' silks on the cos-ter's carts,____ Em – mie a pull-ing her skirt

Ending

an' mut-ter-ing, 'A bal-loon, a bal-loon, I wants__ a bal-loon',__

The__ mis-sus... an' your fa-ther fight-ing: You'll__ wait... that's wot

I wants to know!__ Tabs'll... for – ty – eight bat-ta-lion,

The__ Yel-low... leg up on the path to glo-ry; Now with... Ar-my

of the Marne, An'__ all the time... two men look-ing af-ter bus-iness.

The__ pa-dre... muv-ver 'as you 'ere.'__ An'__ last time... sep-er-y-tion

mon-eys reg'-lar. But__ wy-'r we 'ere, wy-'r we 'ere— that's wot I wants to know?

2nd CHANT

A—— Brass-hat... world an' the Es - ta - mi - nay's daugh - ter,

In a py - ja - ma'd... an Es - ta - mi - na - y cock, An'— I was pinch'd...

with a pint of peas.— And the hens... a place of de - so - la - tion!

3rd CHANT

The— per - ky... queers me, Furi - ous - ly feel - ing... front - line fight - ing.

In his full - blown,... mur - mur, 'Here's a stand - fast... whis - per 'yes - sir'.

Like a bride,... ser - mon, From the cush - y... Tom - my's back - side.

4th CHANT

Jazz - ing back to his ho - tel he now goes gai - ly, Shel - ter'd

and safe where the clock ticks tame - ly. His— back - side warm - ing

a cu - shion, down - fill'd, Green - clad, well splash'd with gold birds red - beak'd.

His— last dim... ju - dy; Cud - dling with proud... the mud of the tren - ches.

His— tu - nic... pass - ing, Through col - our... shop snug in Bond Street.

Shame and scorn... com - pa - ny; Then— the decor - a - tions... of self - sac - ri - fice.

5th CHANT

A——— warn - ing... give,— To the front... do, to God.—

God, un - chang - ing,... night sky To— mask... His self - slay - ing chil - dren.

Stum - bling, swift - ly... grous - ing, Through mud... seek slow the front line.

Squeals of hid - den... wound - ed — Christ who bore... tied to a field gun.

103

THE ENEMY HAS BROKEN THROUGH

The e - ne - my has bro - ken through, bro - ken

through, bro - ken through! Ev - ery man born of wo - man to the

guns, to the guns. To the guns, to the guns, to the guns! Those at

prayer, all in bed and the swil-lers drink-ing deep-ly in the pubs. To the

guns, to the guns. All the bat - men, ev - ery cook, ev - ery

bit - ch's son that hides A whiff of cour - age in his veins, Shel - ter'd

vig-our in his bo-dy, That can run, or can walk, ev - en crawl— Dig him

out, dig him out, shove him on— To the guns!

SONG TO THE GUN

Hail, cool - hard - en'd tow'r of steel em - boss'd

With the fev - er'd, fig - ment thoughts of man;

Guard-ian of our love and hate and fear, Speak for us to the in - ner

ear of God! We be - lieve in God and we be - lieve in thee.—

WOULD GOD, I SMOK'D

Would God, I smok'd_____ and walk'd and
Would God, I smok'd_____ and lift - ed
To hang here ev - en a lit - tle
If you creep to rest in a clos'd - up
Each spar - row, hop - - - ping, ir - re -

watch'd_____ The dance of a gol - den Brim - stone but - ter -
car - goes._____ From the la - den_____ shoul - ders of Lon - don's riv - er -
lon - ger Loung - ing_____ through_____ fear - swell'd, anx - ious
cof - fin,_____ A tail of_____ com - rades see - ing you safe
-spon - si - ble, Is in - den - tur'd_____ in God's migh - ty mem - o -

- fly,_____ To the sau - cy pipe_____ of a
- way;_____ The_____ ho - li - day'd, roar - ing out_____
mo - ments; The_____ hin - der - parts_____ of The
home;_____ Or a ker - nal lost_____ in a
- ry;_____ And we, more_____ than they all, shall_____

green - finch rest - ing In a drow - sy, bram - bl'd lane in
cour - age and move - ment To the_____ mus - cl'd ma - chines of
God of bat - tles Sha - ding our war - tir'd_____ eyes from his
shell ex - plod - ing It's all, sure,_____ on - ly in a
not be lost_____ In the for - get - ful - ness of the

Cum - ber - land._____ In Cum - ber - land._____
Tot - ten - ham Hot - spur. Of Tot - ten - ham Hot - spur.
flam - ing face._____ From his flam - ing face._____
life - - - time._____ A life - - - time._____
Lord of Hosts._____ Of the Lord of Hosts._____

SURGEON'S SONG

Stret - ched on the couch, Jess - ie fon - dl'd her dress, That
hid___ all her beau - ties just o - - ver the knee; And I
won - der'd and said,___ as I sigh'd,___ 'What a shame, that there's
no___ room at all___ on the couch___ there for me.'

STRETCHER-BEARER'S SONG

Oh,___ bear it gent - ly,___ car - ry it soft - ly— A bul - let or a shell said
stop, stop, stop. It's___ had its day,___ and it's left the play, Since it
gam - boll'd o - ver the top, top, top. It's___ had its day___ and it's
left the play, Since it gam - boll'd o - - - ver the top.